Advance Praise

"Ron Stotts gets to the heart of the leadership journey in this wonderful book: As we gain power, authority and fame we must become more diligent, aware and responsible through intentional work on transmuting our unconscious, negative patterns. Stotts shows how those who neglect this foundational work, "not only destroyed their own life but the lives of others who had trusted them." Much more than a guide to "time management" it's a compelling appeal to successful leaders, and to those who desire success, to do the self-healing work required to lead intelligently, effectively and constructively. And, best of all, Stotts provides wise practical guidance to help the reader in this quest."

~**MICHAEL J. GELB**, author of *How to Think Like Leonardo da Vinci* and *The Art of Connection: 7 Relationship Building Skills Every Leader Needs Now*

"Ron Stotts has clearly tapped into "Big Mind" to write this book. It's a brilliant and refreshing deeper look into ourselves."

~**GRAND MASTER DAVE WHEATON**

"You're going to love this book! Dr. Ron Stotts is an amazing guide and role model for awakening and success at a soul level. There are no words to describe my appreciation for Ron and his work... He completely changed my life."

~**TAMARA GERLACH**, Author of *Cultivating Radiance*

"In an age where we are constantly striving to do more to be successful, thought leaders and visionaries are not exempt from 'overscheduling' ourselves. While our intentions seem pure, many of us sacrifice our own health and relationships to serve others. Dr. Ron Stotts playfully and honestly hones in on how we are getting in our own way and gives us the steps we need to expand our time to tackle that next dream project. If you are a transformational leader who is feeling a niggle – or if you are curious about what that is – pick up this book!"

~**RITU GOSWAMY**, Esq., Author of *The New Billable Hour: Bill More Hours, Be More Productive, and Still Have Work-Life Balance*

"Dr. Stotts holds nothing back in this powerful, action-oriented book based on years of working with successful leaders from around the world. The proven success strategies in this book will certainly give you more time while also taking your life and your work to the next level, especially if you think you're too tired or busy to read it."

~**MELODEE MEYER**, #1 bestselling author of *Black Belt Power* and *Clean Food Diet.*

Overscheduled *by* SUCCESS

Over
scheduled
by SUCCESS

A Guide for Influential Leaders
Too Busy to Create Their Next Dream

DR. RON STOTTS

NEW YORK

LONDON • NASHVILLE • MELBOURNE • VANCOUVER

Overscheduled by Success

A Guide for Influential Leaders Too Busy to Create
Their Next Dream

© 2019 Dr. Ron Stotts

Published in New York, New York, by Morgan James Publishing in partnership with Difference Press. Morgan James is a trademark of Morgan James, LLC.
www.MorganJamesPublishing.com

ISBN 9781642791778 paperback
ISBN 9781642791785 case laminate
ISBN 9781642791792 eBook
Library of Congress Control Number: 2018907838

Cover and Interior Design by:
Chris Treccani
www.3dogcreative.net

Morgan James is a proud partner of Habitat for Humanity Peninsula
and Greater Williamsburg. Partners in building since 2006.

Get involved today! Visit
MorganJamesPublishing.com/giving-back

To my wife Carol:
As we have created our lives together, so have we created this book.

We're a great team, and I love you dearly.

To our two great grandsons, Cayden and Alder:
May your lives be a wondrous journey of Self-discovery and awakening.

Table of Contents

Preface

Writing this book has been like introducing myself to who I've become. It's been a good process. I have done my best to learn and grow from all that life has brought me. That has been very challenging at times but has turned out to be quite a rewarding path. I sincerely believe that everything that comes into our life has the potential to be a perfect gift that can help us to heal and more fully open our heart.

Change, for me, is opportunity. It's like the movie *Groundhog Day* with Bill Murray; our ever-changing life gives us countless opportunities to improve how we live, as well as to serve and support others in enjoying their life more fully. It's really all about perspective, and our perspective on and experience of life is the direct result of our level of consciousness. Our level of consciousness is, in a sense, our level of awareness of all that we are, all we can be, and all that life offers. The quieter our mind, the greater our awareness can be. From within that quiet place, we are able to recognize and stay focused on our highest intention, which results in a deeply meaningful life.

I am writing this book to an audience that, I presume, keeps up with or is at least familiar with much of the current brain and science research. In the spirit of keeping this book brief so as to not further burden my busy reader, I have not included elaborate explanations about material that I presume they already understand. My intention in writing this book is to share with thought leaders a proven process I've used with thousands to resolve their challenges and raise their consciousness.

As the world gets busier and noisier, the best way for me to make a significant, positive impact is to offer myself as a supportive guide to those influential leaders. In living life on the leading edge, a common challenge that many share is that they've become over-scheduled by their own success. They're already juggling so much, and those incessant work demands tend to cut into their self-care. It also seems there's not enough time to nurture their most significant relationship, or to dedicate to that next book or special project that's really important to them. These leaders sense they're being called to step up their game, not only for themselves, but also for that bigger contribution they'd like to make.

Yet what if your next book or project isn't something you can create from the busy level of awareness you are currently working from? I know it sure feels like time is the ultimate limitation. And while freeing up time for what's most important may be your main focus, (and we certainly do accomplish that), there's a whole life upgrade that goes along with this inward shift, that turns out to be the real game-changer.

As I guide these leaders to even higher levels, they in turn, influence millions of others in leading more conscious, creative, responsible lives. This is the change we need to see. This is our movement and now is our moment. The world is waiting…

Chapter 1

The Success and Time Predicament

"There cannot be a crisis next week. My schedule is already full."
–Henry Kissinger

We are on the cusp of one of the most evolutionary periods in humankind's history. The success of that evolution, the degree to which we evolve, depends on you.

You've worked hard to create a successful business and a masterful life. The great news is that your work is positively influencing your community and changing lives. The challenge is that, as a result of all your success and the ever-present demands it entails, you may find that you just don't have the time you need to take care of yourself as well as you'd like. Your partner may be wanting to have you around more and is looking for an even deeper connection in your relationship. And that special project that you've been meaning to get to just keeps being set aside. Keeping all these balls in the air has you over-committed and bound to this busy process. Maintaining your successful business requires a lot from you and certainly consumes a tremendous amount of your time. That's a very real and unfortunately all too common predicament, considering that time is the only non-renewable resource!

You may be finding that you don't have time to take care of yourself in the way you'd like. Perhaps you're not getting all of the exercise you'd like, or maybe you find that stress has you eating a bit more – and storing a bit more – than you intended. Although you know the importance of adequate sleep, those restful hours regularly get dwindled down by staying up late to get your next presentation ready, running half-empty on the heels of the last project you just completed. It's no wonder you often don't feel as vibrant or plugged in as you'd like to. Expecting to have a lot of energy isn't an entirely realistic expectation when you're too often burning the candle at both ends.

I do understand your challenge, and you're not alone. It is a problem that naturally goes hand-in-hand with significant success, fame, and business growth. You want to have the influence, you welcome the growth, and yet sometimes the demands on you can feel draining or become distracting, rather than invigorating your business and your life.

This is exactly what happened to Joe – a prominent and influential lifestyle coach. Joe's team, his clientele, and his net worth soared in the mid-2000s, as he gained popularity and notoriety amidst a very receptive crowd. Joe was a marketing genius. In fact, he did so many things well and confidently, that many were shocked at his eventual downfall. I wasn't. I predicted it very early on. Not that I ever put out negative thoughts or expectations toward anyone. My mission is to help influential leaders succeed, to support them in taking their life and work up to the next level. And as they do they, in turn, pass along even more value to their tribe. It can't be otherwise, because when you're playing, seeing, and serving on a higher level, you're influencing with so much more than just what you offer and teach. You are transforming and mentoring through who you are. That's just the way it all works.

Anyway, I saw early on that Joe was ignoring crucial pieces of his life, that I knew would inevitably come back to bite him in the butt. He didn't see it, though. And he didn't want to see it. Joe was far too busy being successful – keeping everything going and growing – to slow down long enough to notice the train wreck in process that was his career and his life. Any observations, offers, or overtures of support I made were simply avoided or ignored. Joe felt like he had things all figured out, and that anyone else's perspective or input was a waste of his time.

His business was bursting at the seams; multi-level high-ticket programs, international retreats, speaking engagements, book deals – Joe's life looked nothing short of enviable and impressive from the outside, yet it was silently eroding from within. Joe and his own staff had him doing so much and going so fast, that none of them paid attention to the huge toll this would take.

As his business grew and grew, it seemed that Joe was always marketing, building, and raising his own bar – often to the exclusion of him paying attention to his students – many of whom had come a long way and spent a lot of money to work with him. And while some of his long-term and dedicated students did become disillusioned and move on, Joe just pushed ever harder with outreach and publicity to attract new followers and enthusiasts.

As his popularity soared, Joe's neglect of his students, even the newer ones, grew. He had such a busy schedule, and so many pieces to attend to in his various programs, events, and appearances, that he simply wasn't paying attention to crucial details. Joe ignored critical elements like "Do my students and staff have enough training to safely and successfully do what I am asking them to do?" Time and terrible outcomes proved that they didn't. It had been Joe's responsibility to train his students and provide the appropriate amount of supervised challenge for them to practice the new skills and concepts he was teaching. It was also vitally important for Joe to watch and listen for feedback as they ventured into new territory. He did neither.

He was too busy, too tired, and too overscheduled to notice. Joe's business imploded, along with his original vision to uplift and do no harm. Sometimes we seriously underestimate the cost of being too busy. And after-the-fact is often too late. I've witnessed this in so many fields, from personal growth to spiritual gurus, and certainly in the business and entertainment fields as well.

Enough about Joe's sad story. Let's talk about you. I know you are conscientious and paying attention to your business and your clientele. That's how you've come so far already. You're a high-integrity player. You take care of your students and your staff. You acknowledge and support the people who support you. In fact, that's even part of what keeps you so busy! Although it was the case for Joe, the casualties of being overscheduled are not always our career or our clients. It's often ourselves that we neglect the most.

Let's look within for a quick personal assessment. Take a moment and really look; be honest with yourself. How healthy are you? How well rested do you feel? Are you enjoying this whole process (which actually is your life), or is it all so demanding that it's been taking a toll on you, your happiness, and your overall wellbeing? There's not only your own care, but perhaps your family or life partner may be wanting more of your time and an even deeper level of connection. And while it may feel a bit "off" to acknowledge that your loved ones wanting more of you is stressful, it is! There's so much you need to do, just to maintain what you've already got going on. And don't forget about those new and bigger dreams of yours that just keep getting put off, again and again. This is the juicy stuff that calls to you! Who has time for all that?

You started out wanting to make a difference and hopefully help a few folks out. You came up with programs and processes, tools, and techniques, and ways to help people enjoy a happier and more successful life. You've become the leader of a community that looks to you to guide them on their way. You're always inventing that next doorway that you will open to them and invite them through. And as much as you love what you do, you find yourself being overscheduled by your own success.

Paul's story:

I am reminded of Paul, a well-known personal development leader in the 80s and 90s. Paul led motivational workshops for people wanting to find and live their purpose and passion. From the outside looking in, it appeared that Paul had become an overnight success, but that was not at all the case. Paul had been sharing his mission for over a decade when he wrote a very popular book that skyrocketed him to guru status in his field.

Although this new level of success, income, and recognition seemed like his dream come true, it brought a new host of challenges into Paul's life. His time became very much in demand, as he had more speaking and book signing offers than he could handle. His workshops and seminars sold out quickly, and it was clear he needed help, as his former small-scale business was getting out of control.

Paul hired a whole team of people to grow and manage it all, yet he knew that it was the wise business person who remained involved in all important aspects of the business – from finance to seminar content and delivery, and from personal contacts to big vision planning. Paul was busy! And within each piece that he did delegate, there were always some hiccups. The AV team didn't create the slides with images and content that really fulfilled his vision. The event management company he hired kept trying out "improvements" that threw Paul off his game. His new financial team struggled to find their flow as business was growing in leaps and bounds, and new policies had to be put into place. With every mistake, Paul took complete responsibility. The more involved he was, the fewer mistakes they made.

And, while Paul's new staff did take a lot off his plate, they still needed quite a bit of his time and input. Paul was trying to get his next book written and was committed to it being a real game-changer. But he had so much going on, he really couldn't devote the time and attention to the book that was required to stay in the flow that was needed to write it. With the constant daily demands of details and decisions that needed to be made, Paul also wasn't able to maintain that expanded consciousness state necessary to write that breakthrough book he envisioned.

The work became a burden, even though Paul was doing what he was passionate about. His once-inspiring vision of writing this special book gradually turned into a task rather than a treat. The whole situation – of committing to do something and then not doing it – felt way out of character for Paul. It was even a source of embarrassment after a while and he found himself hoping that friends and colleagues would not ask him about it. This next book had become an "open loop" that he just didn't see how he was ever going to close. He cared too much about making that contribution to just drop the book idea all together, yet it was not really something he could even get help with, much less delegate.

Something just had to give, so Paul brought on a business partner to carry some of the load. His new partner, Sarah, was incredibly sharp and business savvy, and eager to learn. At first, she breathed new life into Paul's business with her enthusiasm and new ideas. Sarah had a total go-getter attitude. Their styles, though very different, were also quite complementary. As Sarah learned the ropes, she absolutely took many of the organizational responsibilities off Paul's hands and, in fact, handled most even better than he had. Paul was delighted and was sure that this new arrangement would most certainly solve his time crunch. But the honeymoon period was short-lived.

Paul, and his first book, and the seminars that stemmed from it, were still wildly popular, and with Sarah's help, the business grew even faster. With all of this new exposure, Paul had the opportunity to serve so many more people – which was a real blessing – but there was that other side again: being overbooked by his own success. Paul and Sarah had to hire even more help to manage the flood of people who signed up for all of Paul's programs and events.

Sarah was great at booking Paul on prestigious keynote speaking gigs and was even largely responsible for Paul branching out to corporate trainings and consulting. Sarah even managed to book Paul on some high-profile television shows. It seemed that the world couldn't get enough of Paul.

But Paul was hitting a wall. He'd had more than enough. In fact, Paul was becoming overwhelmed in the busyness of his own success and the expectations that everyone else had of him. His very adept team helped him become so popular, in part, by overscheduling him. It seemed to Paul that he was spending half his life in an airport or on the go for some live training or another, and that with the other half of his life, he was running as fast as he could to keep up with all of these engagements. Even though Paul was essentially talking about the same content, no matter who his audience was, each required unique preparation and Paul's full attention.

As the business owner, besides feeling ultimately responsible for any of his team's missteps, Paul experienced another type of pressure from being so very public now. Any mistakes or sub-par deliveries would most certainly be noticed and very publicly too. And while Paul was not afraid of criticism – even welcoming his client's critiques and feedback – there was certainly the added stress of being very much in the limelight. Just look at the magazine covers at all the checkout stands if you don't believe me!

Public or not, Paul set very high standards for himself and was committed to giving 110% with everything he did. The problem was, that over time, he no longer had 110% to give without taking energy and attention away from something else – and that something else was himself.

Paul used to have a personal trainer, and a personal chef preparing and bringing in really healthy meals, but he no longer had time to fit in the regular workouts and traveling forced many meals out with limited choices. So, Paul's waist grew as his workout time shrunk.

Before all of this success, Paul regularly enjoyed a peaceful and restorative 7½-8 hours of sleep. Now he was more often than not up late putting the finishing touches on some workbook or slide presentation for an upcoming event. Even when he did get to bed at a reasonable hour, Paul frequently lay awake in the wee morning hours, constructing the next level of trainings in his head while dreaming of the big impact he wanted to create in the world.

That was the first time that Paul seriously considered seeking outside help. He did have a very big vision and recognized he couldn't get out of his own way to fulfill it. Paul later told me that his initial rationalization for not reaching out for help was that he felt it would be just one more thing on his plate that he didn't have time for. But he later acknowledged several deeper concerns that are very common among highly visible leaders and public figures. Thoughts such as: "What would people think if they knew I didn't have it all together?"

Being a prominent public figure, Paul assumed that people, and his own tribe especially, had the expectation that he had everything under control, that he was always at the top of his game, and that he could solve any problem or issue in a moment, without help, because he's the guy with all the answers. What a trap that was! Also, Paul knew that there's little sympathy for such high-class problems when he had the fame, fortune, and following that others thought they could only dream of. Whatever challenges he had, Paul felt that he should be able to solve them for himself and be that steady, consistent leader who is always there to guide others. That's a pretty heavy (and unrealistic) expectation, but it's the one that Paul convinced himself was true.

With all of Paul's early successes, he and his wife, Shelia, shared all that joy and excitement together. But after the first year or so, their time together shrank as Paul's work demands grew. Shelia realized this was not going to be a "just for now" or "just until" situation. This was their new life and she wasn't very happy about it.

Shelia and Paul rarely had quality time together anymore and, when they did, Paul often seemed preoccupied with something work-related. And while Paul absolutely loved his wife and would do anything for her, it was really kind of stressful for him to sit on the couch and watch a movie together. Paul admitted that as a new idea for his book filtered in or some program deadline hung over him, he would feel angst and want to follow through on that pull. Their need for togetherness didn't quite match, but Paul genuinely wanted to support his wife and her desire to spend quality time with him. Without her, all that he had created would feel pretty lonely and empty.

Running really fast and just out of reach – this is how Paul's life was feeling at that time. And despite all the tools and strategies he had, some of which he had created and most of which he taught to others, he could not get himself off the rat wheel of success – the one of his own making.

Paul just felt like this movement he'd created now had a momentum of its own. He believed that if he cut back or delegated any further, things would fall apart. He believed that balls would drop, people would lose interest, he'd let his clients down, and the movement would suffer. Paul also recognized that there were a lot of people on his team whom he cared deeply about - people who had put their heart and soul into making this movement work. He knew that if he cut out certain aspects of his programs, in order to free up more time for himself, that it would also mean letting some of those talented and committed team members go. They had become like family, and Paul was dedicated and loyal to them, as they were to him.

Paul finally consulted me about three years into this quandary. I'd say it was really his next book that got him to talk to me. Well, that and getting sick an awful lot. Plus, he just wasn't having as much fun with his work as he used to. Things weren't really bad, they just clearly weren't flowing anymore. Paul was well aware that he had become overscheduled by his own success.

Being the sharp guy that he is, Paul recognized that he was simply too enmeshed in the situation to see it all clearly. Though he initially hesitated to get completely real with me, in asking questions, as is my way, it became clear that privacy and anonymity were super important to Paul. I assured him that he absolutely had that with me. I have worked with thousands of people in many different countries – some famous, and many being notable leaders in their industry or profession. I acknowledged to Paul that anonymity is an essential part of what makes our work together work.

I noticed Paul take a deep breath and drop his guard as I explained that, for me, it is knowing that we are in a safe, supportive place, that makes it comfortable enough to explore the deeper levels within ourselves and say whatever comes up. It's that confidentiality that gives us the safety to venture beyond our known comfort zone and journey deeper within ourselves than we have, perhaps, ever gone before.

Paul began to appreciate that I was like a guide who was very familiar with the areas that he wanted to explore. He began to realize that he was the real explorer, and that I was just there to make sure he found what he was looking for and returned home safely. We had to trust each other as I asked him supportive questions that would help him find his own best answers. Those answers, of course, revealed his path. I was just there holding the flashlight, so he could find his way.

This is exactly what Paul and I did together, and it worked! No surprise there. After a very short time, Paul was once again truly inspired by his work. He finished his next book, got it published, and it became another bestseller, all within that same year. His new book did exactly what he had hoped it would – it opened up a whole new area of interest for his readers and allowed Paul to develop the more specific focus that had been calling him. His new book created a whole new awareness for his tribe. All of Paul's worries – that if he wrote about this new subject, his tribe might not follow – were all for naught. In fact, Paul realized that he wasn't giving his followers enough credit. They wanted to grow and evolve every bit as much as he did. By Paul stepping out of what he believed was his expected realm of expertise, he gave his clients both the permission and the path they needed to deepen their own personal growth journey. Turns out that his higher-level students also began making richer contributions to others in their work and lives – just as Paul had envisioned they would.

In retrospect, Paul realized that one thing that had been holding him back from writing his book was a pitfall that he knew very well. He realized he had been getting hung up on the "what" and the "how" rather than staying focused on his end goal. Ironic, I know, being a personal development leader himself.

We both had a good chuckle over that one. As I always say, "If you can't laugh at yourself, you're taking it all much too seriously!"

As for Paul's relationship with his wife, it too, seemed to simultaneously deepen as Paul did his own inner work. With Paul doing the inner work and becoming who he needed to be to write that next book, he became the deeper, and more present, aware, and sensitive partner that Shelia was wanting from him.

Paul was very taken with the spiraling up effect that occurred in our work together. As he described it, "The more things worked, the more things worked!" My work is really about getting your inner being and your whole life in alignment, and supportively using the delightful and powerful flow that ensues when you do.

The truth is that, whether you're running a successful Mom and Pop operation, or a billion-dollar industry, you are likely to run into feelings of being overwhelmed and not having enough time at each stage of your business' evolution. At every level of growth, you have been working within certain perspectives, constraints, and ways of doing business that you are familiar with. Of course, any outer change will require some inner change from you. What used to work was great for then, but not for now, as you and your business evolve into new phases.

When you are feeling like you don't have enough time, or perhaps are even overwhelmed by the strain and stress that your success has created, it is time to make a shift. It's time to look at what you and your business need, so that you can make that shift and step into the next level of success. You intuitively know that this is what's needed and is what would benefit both you and your clients. If you're feeling uncomfortable with this higher level of challenge in your business, then I congratulate you.

This challenge is both an indicator of your success, and a clear indicator of your opportunity to grow. Your "problem" is the neon billboard on your front lawn, as I jokingly refer to it. It's merely your life telling you that it's time to expand your vision for yourself and for the next stage of your business. You asked for more, and now it's here.

What you may at first see as a problem is really just a part of doing business, and the great news is that each of these perceived problems is really a wonderful opportunity. You know that, but it's sometimes hard to remember when you're right in the middle of it. I remember the summer after I turned sixteen; when I was away from home and digging ditches for a pipeline, I grew six inches and had to get all new clothes. While your current business growth challenge is not quite so simple, it is kind of like that. You're growing, and the "clothes" just don't fit any more.

What do you need to change? How do you need to do things differently? What tools or techniques do you need so that you can do your work more efficiently and effectively? That's what we're taking a look at in this book. Each chapter will guide you into another level of resolving and benefitting from your once-problems, now-opportunities. We'll start with the more obvious and move into the less familiar (but even more valuable).

If you're feeling overscheduled by success, then read on to learn about how you can create the time and the opportunity you need to enjoyably handle your business while also taking better care of yourself, your relationships, that special project, or whatever it is you dream of next.

Chapter 2

It's an Inside Job

"If someone else is spending your time, then it's time for a change."
—Ron Stotts

Overscheduled and not enough time:

As we acknowledged in chapter one, you are overscheduled by your own success. This means the first thing we want to take a look at is how you are using your time. This is the chapter that I know you could do a great job writing yourself - if you had time. So, let me go over the basics for you, just in case you've gotten so tangled up in what you're doing that you have forgotten what you know that you know.

Please keep in mind that when we're referring to how you're spending your time, we are actually talking about how you are spending your life. So always keep in mind what your highest purpose and intentions are for your life. Staying focused on your highest intention gives you clarity and makes your decisions easier. Whatever doesn't support your highest intention isn't something that you want to invest your time or life in. So, first take a look at your current projects and goals to see how they fit into your bigger picture. Then review your upcoming projects and new dreams and see if they are also in alignment with your highest intention.

A huge time saver that can open up your schedule is letting go of projects that just don't support your greater purpose. I appreciate that you're a very creative and multi-talented person. It's because you're good at so many things that the temptation is always there to just do this or that project that "really won't take much time at all." You also may be overextending yourself out of your desire to help and support others, or perhaps your team members want to involve you in their pet projects. What could it hurt to take a bit more of your time and give it to others? The answer, as you well know, is that it can affect your health, relationships, and drain you – not necessarily in any big or dramatic way – but just enough so that you aren't in the best consciousness to get that special project done, and to stay focused on your highest intention.

Managing a project:

So, with that said, let's dive into ten top time-management strategies, to help you stay focused and get things done.

1. **Plan out the project:**
   It's common to want to get started on a project and just figure it out as you go. But having a clear big picture of who your specific audience or customer is, what you are specifically offering them, and the desired end results that you're looking for are basics that need to be clear from the beginning. You can then more efficiently plan out your project with those parameters in mind.

2. **Bite sizes are easier to chew:**
   Once you have the big picture of the project clearly laid out, the next thing to do is to break it down into smaller pieces that are more defined and feel doable to team members who are involved.

It's that old, "How do you eat an elephant?" thing that people used to joke about. If each aspect of the project is further broken down into smaller chunks, then people don't tend to get so overwhelmed and resistant.

3. **Time estimates:**

   Start with looking at each of the bite-size pieces of the project and estimate, as best you can, how long each of those will take. Then, looking at the larger sections or aspects of the project, add the bite-size times up and see if you've allotted enough time for that particular segment. Then, of course, add up each segment and see if the overall time allotment is reasonable and worth your investment. Does it work financially and logistically? Do you have the team and the time to commit to the project, allowing for those little changes and enhancements that will surface during the process?

4. **Start and complete dates:**

   When do you want to start the overall project, and when do each of the components or modules of the project need to begin so that it all cohesively comes together in the end? Keep in mind that this timetable will influence your team members, for better or for worse. If the timing is too tight or unreasonable, then you'll likely experience subconscious, if not conscious, resistance from the team. You may even feel a little resistance showing up within yourself.

5. **Prepare your work space:**

   Just as you'd do if you were going to build a boat or landscape a yard, you want to make sure that your workspace, and the overall environment that's involved, is prepared. You'll want to have everything you need on hand, so there are fewer delays. This is a good time to make *To Do* lists for the overall project, for every project segment, and for each of those doable little tasty bites of your elephant.

6. **Choosing your team:**

   Who do you need on your team to make sure that you can get this project done within the time frames that make it work for you? Can you handle it alone, with your existing team, or do you need to bring in other people or even specialists to help with the workload? Choose your players well so that you're focused and getting the most out of your time. If you don't feel like you can totally trust the team to do a great job with their part of the project, then you're more likely to end up micromanaging out of necessity. Do you really have the time or even want to be doing that?

7. **Getting on the same page:**

   It is critical that you and each of your team members are crystal clear about the overall project, what each person needs to do, and how their part of the project fits into the bigger picture. Delegate everything that you can to the people you know can be responsible for getting their job done. You're the big-picture person, and they need to be helping you create your masterpiece, not off doing their own thing. Everyone needs to be on the same page and contributing to the same story.

8. **Dealing with the unexpected:**

   Yes, there will be the unexpected, and the best way to deal with it is to expect it ahead of time. You can create your best plan ever, but it will mature and evolve as the project moves along. And that's a good thing. When we're present in the creative process, the project and our lives can be enhanced in unexpectedly delightful ways. There are times when you will want to embrace the change – trusting it and going with the flow.

9. **The gifts of procrastination:**

   If or when you feel some piece of the project is stalling, take a moment and see how you're feeling and what it is that may be going on. If it feels like you have a team member who is procrastinating, it could well be because they aren't clear about what they need to be doing. That could mean that there is a lack of clarity in the project itself and that would be something that needs your attention. You can also always break a more challenging area of the project into smaller pieces to help with clarity.

10. **Breathe and Enjoy:**

    I don't want to sound too new-age-y here, but if you find yourself not breathing or enjoying the project, then you will want to take a moment and get yourself back into a better state of consciousness. It may be the perfect time for a fill-you-up break. Your level of consciousness will be mirrored in the team and reflected in the quality of the project. I really can't emphasize this enough.

If you feel like you have been using these or other similar strategies to resolve your challenges of being overscheduled by success, then let's look a little deeper for how to resolve your challenges.

Go in, find out:

I'm betting that on some level you know that, at your age, you really can't afford to not take care of yourself. I'm also presuming that you know how important it is to make sure your partner isn't feeling left out of your life. I'll even go out on a limb here and bet that deep down you recognize that, in order to get more time to take care of yourself, to more deeply connect with your partner, and to get that special project done, you have to let go of something that is holding you back. You probably even know, at some level, that you need to make a real shift in your life. Maybe you're worried how your partner, team, or clients will deal with yet another change. But I bet you at least suspect that, if you could just do what it takes to make this shift, you'd become the person who can easily and enjoyably handle it all.

I absolutely recognize that you actually are overbooked due to your own success. I get it, your team is overscheduling you, and you really don't have the time to handle everything that's on your plate. You're doing everything you can just to keep up with the goals and commitments that you already have. I fully appreciate, understand, and acknowledge that this is the problem that you are having.

This is exactly the challenge that my friend and colleague, a busy publisher and single mom, recently shared with me. Amanda described how the more successful she and her business became, the busier she got. She explained how, in a genuine attempt to resolve her time crunch, she reworked her schedule and hired a new full-time person in order to free up a whopping 36 hours every week that she wanted to dedicate to working with her highest-level clients. While Amanda was able to free up the exact amount of time that was her goal, she found herself quickly filling up that time with all kinds of other activities. She just wasn't able to get herself to devote that time to her higher priority intention that she thought she really wanted. So, while Amanda had managed to carve out the time, she had not cleared up her underlying resistance – the real reason she was not engaging on a more powerful level in her work and in her life. Once she saw this, she jumped in and did the work, which allowed her to step up her entire game. I knew she would – Amanda's a total rock star!

From her higher place of personal evolution, Amanda has enjoyed spending the majority of her time engaged with her top-level authors, guiding them into their own brilliant expression and success. Amanda's story is a classic case of what happens when we haven't looked deeper within and acknowledged and resolved the real source of our problem – and, how great things turn out when we do.

While I can promise you that I can help you with your challenge, this is likely going to look different than you thought it would. With you being a successful leader, I imagine that you are training others to be able to do what you do. You are the teacher and your students are preparing to one day be able to take over aspects of what you have been doing and training them to do for years. And, as a true master, I know that you hope they will not only reach your level of mastery, but exceed it. Just as a good parent wants their children and their children's children to be better and better parents, as the master, you want the same for those learning from you.

As you apply the ten tools I shared in the beginning of this chapter, you may be happy to see how they can help you get rid of some of the symptoms of feeling and being overbooked. You've organized, delegated, and leveraged your time so that you can handle what's on your plate and still have room for dessert. There are any number of tools and techniques for time management, and I bet you have used as many or more than most people have. Heck, you may have even invented a bunch of them! The question is: Why aren't they working to the extent that you need them to at this level of play?

The answer to that question is that the myriad of methods that you can read about in a dozen or more books, all tend to focus on you dealing with just the symptoms of your not having enough time. It's like the overweight person who is told about this or that diet they should follow to lose weight. They try it and, low and behold, it actually works. They do lose weight – for a short time – before they then gain it all back and then some. The problem is identified as being overweight, when, in truth, that is often actually just a symptom of a deeper emotional challenge, one often stemming from either earlier childhood or a later incident in their life, that can only be found by looking deeper within.

I know that you know and understand all of this. All I'm suggesting is that just as the extra weight is only a symptom, so is being overbooked and not having enough time. We can temporarily solve the symptoms with time management techniques and quick fix solutions, but the deeper challenges remain untouched and often just reappear in the same or some other expression.

We can easily resolve those outer symptoms that you are aware of in your life, only to have them reappear. But the real question is: Do you want to identify and heal the deeper source of what is going on so that, like Amanda, you can move fully forward with your life? What level do you want to play on – living with the ever-recurring symptoms, or actually dealing with and healing the deeper inner challenge? By the way, please let me remind you that your inner resolutions hold the gifts and the opportunities for you to be able to enjoy your life while fulfilling your dreams – the old and the new.

So, with you being a master, when I ask, "What level do you want to play on?" I, of course, already know your answer.

A few months ago, I had lunch with a very talented woman who was going to be taking a test for her First-Dan, a mastery test in Hapkido. She felt confident that she could do well in nearly all of the test, except for when using the knife. She shared with me her clever plans as to how she could avoid having to use the knife in the test so she could get the title she sought. I innocently asked, "So you really just want the title of master, not to actually become a master?" The question went unanswered.

But the point is, that a true master looks for those areas of their life that require more focus, and proactively seeks to overcome the limitations that are revealed. As you well know, becoming a master is a life-long journey. It is a way of life. The Hero's Journey is not a one-and-done deal; it's a recurring adventure, each of which takes us deeper within. This is how we find our way out of our challenge and up to a new level of mastery.

There was a well-known actress that I worked with a few years ago who felt that she just wasn't being offered the roles that she deserved and wanted. She was looking outside herself to blame others for and to find solutions to her perceived problem. As we began to look deeper within, she broke down in tears as she recognized that she was actually terrified of the vulnerability and raw emotion that the roles that she was saying she wanted, called for. It took her a bit of breathing, tears, and inner reflection, but I congratulated her on being willing to go through the five-step transformational process that my work involves – trusting that she would come out the other end empowered and truly fearless, regardless of what any role might call for. I was impressed to watch her career unfold over the next few years as she not only took on, but successfully portrayed the deeper, more complex characters she played.

I also saw a corporate version of this when I was VP of Inner Game and working with AT&T during their divestiture. I was working with all levels of management and, from the top down, they were all overwhelmed by all it was going to take to break up their monopoly and successfully compete in the for-profit market. Their primary concern was how, in the limited time they had, were they going to shift management from the decades-old mentality of playing it safe and not rocking the boat, to one where they all had to start thinking outside of the box and taking career risks in order to succeed in the new competitive environment. The secondary challenge they faced was retraining all of their overall-wearing, toolbox-carrying mechanics into khaki-wearing, briefcase-carrying, computer savvy technicians.

As I tactfully explained some of the deeper dynamics of what was truly going on to one of the heads of the company, he realized that it would take top-down modeling of the new behavior in order to accelerate the required corporate-wide shifts. The whole culture of the company had been highly conditioned to be risk-adverse. The classic and well-known scenario in their company had been that if one of them ever tried something new, and it didn't work out, that risk would sideline the rest of their career. Taking a risk could cost them any potential promotions they might have otherwise automatically gotten, had they just shown up and kept their head down.

So, upper management saw how they had to lead the way by thinking outside the box and taking risks before others would follow. Upper management also saw the clear need for them to do some very real inner work in order to win the new outer game, in which their new regional companies could be successful.

I have to say that, after all of the preliminary AT&T research I did for the summary report of what was needed for a successful divestiture, I felt like I could have been talking about any family in America. The company dynamic was like a familiar story that I'd often seen over the years, where Dad was like this and Mom was like that, and so the kids turned out the various ways they did. I shared this analogy with one of the three top leaders in the company, and he totally got it. This shift in his perspective allowed him to recognize that if top-level management did the work, making the shifts in themselves first and leading from a much more functional place, the rest would follow suit. Their original concern of not knowing what to do, how to do it, and feeling like they didn't have time for any of it, fell away. They saw that by making these core shifts within themselves, they would have enough time and be on track for a successful divestiture.

As a doctor of chiropractic and a transformational therapist, I have seen how, over the years, people come in with what they see as the problem – whether that's a relationship, health, spiritual, financial, or mental/emotional challenge. Yet that identified problem is almost always just a symptom. Once they are willing to go deeper within, we can easily find the source of the problem, which then makes it easy to know how to effectively resolve whatever's going on. The next step of their understanding is then how they can supportively modify their life, so that the problem doesn't recur.

Don't tell anyone, but Buddha figured all of this out quite a while ago. He called it *The Four Noble Truths*.

Who's most aware of your inner game?

You know the old saying about, "If you're not watching your money, you can be sure someone else is." Well, that goes for other things as well, like, "If you're not watching your time, your energy, your highest intention, and your life's purpose…" I'm sure that your entire team is consciously doing all that they can to fully support you, and that doing so is always their highest goal. But there is a potential problem in that they are only aware of the 5% of their thoughts that are conscious. What may be going on unconsciously or subconsciously in the other 95% of their thoughts is anyone's guess.

For a person to be aware and consciously managing their subconscious thoughts, they will have had to, in some form or another over the years, fully invest in going through the five steps I'm sharing in this book. That means, that in order for them to best support you, your whole team needs to be playing on a master's level. If you're not sure if they all are, then I know one thing for sure: You have to be. I don't doubt that your people love and support you, and that you need to be holding the reins of your life. You know as well as I do that we can't blame others for overscheduling us. As the responsible and influential leader that you are, it's your game to consciously play.

The spiritual analogy of the master:

A modification of an old classic is that, "Once upon a time, long, long ago, there was a team of powerful horses racing down an old dirt road. The coachman was holding on tight to the reins as the coach careened through the night. Sitting within the coach, there was a messenger who has been asked to take an important message to a distant town."

This story snippet always caught my attention because there was a time as a champion rower in college and as a Marine that I was that powerfully physical team of horses delighting in unleashing that young-man's power. As I moved along with my education, I began to identify more with the driver of the carriage, as I was intellectually determining my life and enjoying the challenges of graduate school. Later, in my mid-twenties, as I was recovering from the realization that I had some deep shit going on in my life, I stepped out of my comfort zone and went on a real Hero's Journey. As I began to resolve deeper issues and began to meditate, my life found some balance and my mind became quieter. With those shifts, I began to see myself more as the person riding within the carriage, who knew where they were going and what the importance of the message was.

The funny thing is, though, that as my path continued to unfold, I realized that I felt more closely connected to the guy who was back at the castle that had sent the messenger out on the journey to the distant town. Of course, I later realized that I was also actually the person who had told the guy at the castle to send the messenger on the journey. It turns out that the deeper we go within, the more we understand that there is always another level. We continue to become the one who is ever-more aware of the bigger picture of the story.

There is likely no starting or end point, just your choice as to what level you want to play on. After all, you are all of it. Remember your decision, years ago, that you would be taking full responsibility for your life? If you are overscheduled by your own success, then what you actually have is a marvelous opportunity. You get to take another look within, going even a little deeper this time, at what distracted you from being as mindful as you know you are. In seeing this snag from the past that has resulted in this life circumstance you identify as being overscheduled, you then have the opportunity to take your life up to the next level. In resolving whatever this inner snag is, you get to be more aware and conscious. This, of course, will be what allows you to better take care of yourself, your relationships, and create that next dream....

The question always is, "What level do you want to play on?" In the next five chapters, I'd like to share with you a path that I can promise will give you back your time, your dreams, and "control" of your life. You will learn how you can choose and live your life from whatever level you'd find most rewarding and enjoyable.

What I will be sharing with you will not only create lasting change, but will allow you to create the change that most fully supports both you and your work. I've used this process with thousands of people over the past 45 years. I've purposely designed it (or I should say, Big Mind has), to provide an upgrade for your whole life. As so many others have experienced, this work brings about an inner shift that will take care of the actual source of your challenges while giving you the energy, the ability, and the vision to gratefully enjoy the rest of your journey.

Chapter 3

Realizing Your Challenges
Are Opportunities

"When it is obvious that the goals cannot be reached, don't adjust the goals,
adjust the action steps."
–Confucius

While change is the one constant that we can count on in our life, it is also what allows for our personal transformation to take place. Life can be moving along smoothly and then we feel a jiggle or a niggle in "the Force." It's as if life is a bowl of Jello and you're one of the pieces of fruit suspended within it. You become aware that your world, your life, is vibrationally shifting. Something is jiggling your comfort zone.

Most people have refined their ability to ignore the jiggles, until the shift sufficiently disrupts their life and the drama finally forces them to wake up enough to see what the heck is going on. If what's going on is too overwhelming or falls in the category of too uncomfortable to look at or deal with, then they go unconscious again, falling back asleep. Instead of living a life of personally expanding, they choose to live a life of contracting and playing ever smaller. They don't want anything to rock the boat of their comfort zone, and they sure as heck don't want to look at any of that emotional crap from the past that might be trying to sneak back into their life again.

I was in a large shopping mall visiting a pet store one day. I could see, way in the back, a family looking at a litter of puppies. As I watched, one of the puppies made a break for it and ran as fast as he could towards the large opening that led into the mall. The store was carpeted and as the pup reached the opening he slammed on the brakes. The mall floor was stone. He sniffed and fussed and barked and wiggled, but that change was just too dangerous and unknown, too scary to risk. Looking back to the safety of his frolicking sister and brother pups, he finally turned and ran for the comfort of the known.

As a new little pup, I'd say that was a good choice, but I see people doing that for their entire life and never really stepping into the life of possibility that awaits them. That unknown is also opportunity; it is the area beyond our comfort zone where life actually begins.

You are, of course, not like most people or that pup who ran for safety. Your life is all about stepping up your game. You didn't get to be an influential leader by ignoring the past and pretending it has no effect on our current or future life. If you were like me, you might have tried that when you were younger, but things just kept coming up, so you decided to do something about it.

I certainly remember getting out of the Marines on a medical discharge and having my dad treat me like I'd violated all of the sacred Boy Scout laws in one fell swoop. I certainly realized that for many people at that time, going to Vietnam and participating in killing anyone you were told to kill (including kids, grandmas, and everybody else that looked different from us), was the normal and acceptable thing to do. But to me, it really didn't feel like the American way. I also realized that I not only didn't really like the idea of killing someone else, but the whole idea of them trying to kill me didn't sit too well either. With all the stories that I was being told by the guys returning, it sounded like the craziest place in the world.

It was late in 1967 and I traded in all of the beliefs and rules that I'd been raised with for a blank slate of "What do I want to believe, and what are the rules that work for the reality that I want to live in?" It was an emotionally difficult time, and finding out that 62 of my friends didn't come back didn't help at all. What's a teenage kid to do? Several years later, after my divorce and my recovery from what turned out to be a chemical imbalance (so much for my *Leave it to Beaver* life), I holed up in a cabin on an island, and stuck my feet into the oven of the wood stove and started reading the Bible and anything else I could find that would help me make sense of this life!

This could have been the worst part of my life, and for some time, I saw it as just that. But, with the 20/20 hindsight that we develop over time, I realized that the worst of times were truly the best of times for me. I was a frickin' mess, no doubt about it. But those extreme times forced me to choose between doing nothing or becoming something. And so, it was then my path consciously began. Thank God for those terrible times, because without them, I would have never gone to the depths of my inner being to rescue and revive the person that I am today. I would have been "Ron the all-American boy," but not the much more interesting, connected, and intricate, examined "me" that I have become. And I like this "me" a whole lot better.

So it is with all the changes that life brings to us. Each and every one of them has the potential for being a gift that is perfectly designed to help us open up our heart and become more whole and complete – just as we were designed to be. These changes – these potentially perfect gifts – help us to remember and restore ourselves to being who we were when we first came in, before the effects of the chemical and social soups that we were bathed in. It's who we were before we realized that we needed to fit in to survive. And to fit in, we felt that we had to act, be, and do how others expected and wanted us to act, be, and do, so that they'd accept and love us.

Our path is one of remembering who we were before we started shutting down and shoving down parts of ourselves that we perceived made others uncomfortable or to even disconnect from us. These "unacceptable" parts became securely locked down, deep in our inner cave. When I was younger and exploring where this path of mine led, there were initially some dark and scary places, that I fortunately learned would always turn out to be the greatest gifts. There were also revealed to me some of the most amazing and magical places that most folks will never even know exist. As my path meandered on and I became more of my authentic self again, the life changes and challenges that I grew through became subtler and subtler.

What used to be a major life-quake was now more like one of those of little jiggles or niggles we mentioned earlier. I had to breathe and be mindful to even recognize them for the gifts they were, or they'd pass by me unnoticed. Of course, those I didn't notice always came back around with a little bigger wallop than they'd had before. But as I learned to trust the perfection of the Universe and appreciate the abundance that we live in, I began to let go and trust the process even more, paying attention to the whispers and staying open to the guidance and gifts that followed.

By making supportive choices, life can become pretty quiet and those niggles get even subtler. That is unless you're in a significant relationship – in which case, your partner tends to always reflect your next opportunity for you – whether you enjoy that or not! Relationship is surely the greatest gift for one who is on the spiritual journey. You really can't ignore or get away with anything. Your relationship with yourself is always clearly mirrored in your relationship with others. And aren't we all just thrilled about that? You may also notice your relationship with yourself reflected in your work life as well.

With the great work you have done on your own path, you are most likely moving well out of the raw drama stage and into the niggles. For instance, being overscheduled by your own success is a niggle. Not taking care of yourself as well as you'd like is definitely a niggle. And not having time to create your next dream is more like a full-fledged wiggle. That dream just keeps flickering inside of you, wanting your attention to nurture it into the bright burning flame you both want it to be.

Just as our more notable challenges can turn out to be wonderful opportunities to notice yet another level of healing that we have available to us, so too can the subtler niggles and wiggles alert us to the same thing. Yes, you can look at what you want or need to change outside of yourself, like in your environment or relationships, or your lifestyle, etc… and that might work out well for a while. But while those outer changes can work on a more surface level, what you are generally doing is just treating a symptom, rather than the deeper source of what is going on.

We are a society that loves to treat symptoms with this or that, and sometimes both. As a matter of fact, the only thing we love more is not looking within at what the deeper source of a niggle, a wiggle, and especially a life-quake may be. The real problem is, while those symptoms might temporarily go away, they soon resurface in some irritatingly disruptive way. Yes, if you weren't who you are, you'd just treat that symptom and then the next and the next, but that is not who and what you are, is it?

You're an influential leader, and so those niggles and wiggles, like being overscheduled by your own success, are music to your ears that gently wake you up and suggest that there is a learning opportunity waiting for you on line one. I know that you know this is true. In your life, when you find yourself not taking as good of care of yourself as you'd like, it is time to pay attention and see what's up. When your partner is asking for more time and a deeper connection with you, it's time to pay attention and recognize you possibly are not being as mindful or heart-centered as you'd like or need to be. When a special project is put off or set aside for a short time while other things get done, that's fine. But when that project gets put off for a year or two or three or more, then you know that it's time to pay closer attention. It's time to go within and check out what's going on.

It may be time to go on a hero's journey down into the depths of your cave, muck around a bit, and see what's not quite as it should be. It's time to go within and find that part of you that got left behind at some point in your life - when something wasn't understood or emotionally dealt with. This is what our collective life traumas are made of. Ignored life traumas lead to internal noise, distraction, and stress. But you can calm that inner stress and distraction by finding that inner place where you got stuck, and getting it unstuck so that you can heal it, love it, and re-integrate it back into your life. Let out the stress and trauma, and let the love and acceptance back in. While at first this may seem elusive or complicated, with practice, over time, it becomes as natural as breathing in and out.

Let this process become an empowering part of all that you are. As you do, you will again be able to breathe fully, be more mindful, and live more in the present. You will be that much more conscious, and that much more aware. You will realize that you no longer feel overscheduled or unable to take care of yourself and your relationship. You will find yourself playing on another level that makes it all an enjoyable adventure again.

I'm just saying, as a conscious, influential leader, you are no doubt breathing and wanting to be mindfully living your life in the present, to the best of your ability. Yet the only way to continue to do that is to handle the niggles that life brings you (preferably before they become life-quakes!). It just makes good sense. It's really the only way to go, yes?

Your Zone of Evolution:

As a successful leader, you are consciously breathing along your personal growth path and enjoying being present during each step, as well as with the quantum leaps that come along unexpectedly. There is a rhythm and a flow to your life that is part of your success. It's tempting for us to be lulled into a sense of comfort that the way it is will also be the way it will continue to be. Sure, you are working hard and maybe traveling too much, but it's all part of the game. And let's face it, as frenzied as it all can feel at times, you're loving playing in the game.

With your busy schedule and many demands, it's easy to excuse yourself for not being able to eat as well as you'd like or not getting as much exercise as you used to. It's easy to feel your partner will understand your being distracted and focused on this and that upcoming event. You can even tell yourself, "I will get back to that special project after this next round of deadlines and events is done." In other words, it's easy to ignore, or not even notice, when the winds of change gently blow in the subtle indicators that opportunities for growth are available.

You are no doubt asking for a fulfilling, successful, and rewarding life. And with each step forward, you are exploring your potential and supporting the growth of others. And, as you expand your world, your consciousness, and your sense of self, you are asking more from and of yourself. That "more" that you are accessing will come, in part, from within yourself.

I'll date myself here, again, but think of a woman wearing an angora sweater, leaning against a stucco wall. As she pulls away from that wall, parts of the sweater will get snagged in the texture of the stucco. This is similar to what happens when we expand and live a "bigger" life.

As a child and while growing up, there are always things that happen that we just don't know how to emotionally process or deal with. It could be as little a thing as having a playmate steal a toy away, or when that boy or girl you have fantasized about talking with turns away and ignores you. It can also be those events like having someone we know die, a parent who is an alcoholic or one who is emotionally unavailable to us, a divorce from a life partner who actually had a lot of personality traits similar to one of your parents. There are the little things, the bigger things, and then, of course, the myriad of moments in the middle, all of which take a toll.

Our emotional backlog isn't always a big event that we are completely aware of. It is oftentimes the thousands of social cuts that turn into scars that can limit our ability to move through life. When those big or little issues rise to the surface as the wiggles and niggles, we sometimes resist them, allowing them to hold us back and take us out of the flow. We need to take a moment – or whatever time it takes – to give attention to the source of what's going on. We need to notice the niggle and then give ourselves whatever we need: be it a full, deep breath, or a deeper look within. We definitely need to breathe, look at what we're feeling, and then at what it is we're needing in that moment. We need to love ourselves enough and give ourselves the time and attention required to release that snag and regain our full range, so we can get on, unencumbered, with our life.

Here's the most important thing that I really want to make sure you understand: Each and every healing opportunity is a gift. Running into your emotional backlog or issues from your past isn't a bad thing. Those are actually wonderful indicators that you are growing and doing well in your life. It's by healing those niggles and wiggles (and yes, the life-quakes) that you are able to grow.

The energy that you were using to keep that emotional challenge in check, once released, can now be used to nurture yourself or invest in that special goal or project. You have taken your foot off the brake pedal and can now experience less resistance and increased forward motion from the gas pedal. That inner healing and resolution gives you access to the special kind of energy you need to expand your consciousness. It also allows you to enrich your work, and to live more mindfully with an abundant and loving attitude.

Change is great. Change by conscious choice results in an aligned life of flow. You have the opportunity to clean up the distractions and the resistances that gnaw away at your life, your health, your enjoyment, and your focus. And when you do eliminate inner resistance and distractions, your whole life shifts in such a way that you are no longer overscheduled or feeling a lack of time. You are back in the flow and ready to go. You are embracing change and gratefully receiving all those perfect gifts that the abundant universe provides. You now recognize and appreciate that the niggles are just indicators – little taps on the shoulder letting you know that you have yet again expanded, and another growth opportunity is available to you. Lucky you! Your zone of evolution awaits.

Of course, you don't have to change:

Nobody forces us to deal with old issues that distract, deplete, and derail us. That's our choice. Being a guy who lives by the ocean and loves boating, there was a YouTube video about lobsters that caught my attention. You've probably seen it, but it's a good metaphor. The lobster is scuttling along in life, enjoying the abundance of its ocean home, when it starts to feel that something isn't quite right.

It's just a niggle to start with, but the feeling grows into a wiggle. What is happening is that the lobster is growing, and no longer fits in its current shell, and it is time for him (or her) to grow a new one. When the lobster feels that inner niggle of expansion, it must first find a good rock to hide under, and then it literally wiggles back out of its shell. It has to let go of the very thing that has protected it and kept it safe. This is really the ultimate letting go, because during this process the lobster is left completely vulnerable. The thing is, though, if it doesn't surrender and endure through that temporary vulnerable period, it will die in the confines of its old limiting shell. Ironically, it is their willingness to be vulnerable that gives them the ability to continue to grow.

Just as that once comfortable and protective shell was just perfect for the lobster, so our comfort zones serve us for a time. And just like the lobster, if we want to grow, then we will need to step out of that now-limiting comfort zone. An early mentor of mine, Joseph Campbell, named this familiar process "The Hero's Journey." Our hero's journey takes place when we either choose to leave or get kicked out of our comfort zone, usually due to some event or change in our life. There we are, relatively naked and vulnerable in a new territory. As we venture forward, we run into unfamiliar things and events that are scary to us.

Joseph referred to those unknown experiences and entities as our demons and dragons. Our first reaction to them is often to either run, to attack and defend ourselves, or to become frozen in inaction. At some time during the fight, we become exhausted enough by our struggle to begin to let down our guard. And, as we do, we start to realize that those perceived demons and dragons are actually our allies or opportunities to grow. They are actually a very valuable part of who and what we are. Remember in an early Star Wars episode when Yoda suggested to Luke that he didn't need to take his lightsaber into the cave? It's kind of like that.

As we recognize and connect with those disparate parts of ourselves, we become more whole and empowered. And just as it is in the classic tales, from that more empowered and conscious place, we journey home and share our story of personal growth, triumph, and discovery that inspires others to go on their own hero's journey.

In other words, it is by wiggling out of our limiting shell that we become capable of evolving and continuing to grow along our journey. As Joseph shares, this story is found within all cultures throughout the centuries. It is the story of how we live and grow and evolve over time. You can choose to ignore your story or just hope that your latest shell will fit perfectly forever. (Good luck with that, by the way.) Or, you can remember and enjoy this amazing process. We get to choose how we want to live our lives – either from a place of contracting fear or from a place of expanding love. We get to choose to either expand our consciousness or contract it. Either way, change will continue to occur. After all, it is the one constant in life.

A choice we all have:

I'm sure, as I mentioned earlier, when those initial indicators surface in your life, it is tempting to try to just take care of the symptoms and hope the deeper challenge will go away. That may work sometimes, or for some time, but it can also be like scratching an itch on a broken arm and hoping that will handle the entire problem.

The very symptoms that we are trying to get rid of are the same valuable indicators that we can and, from my perspective, should be looking forward to. Those symptoms might show up as a challenge in our work, our relationships, or our life. They can be little things that, over time, become bigger things. But regardless, if we are just treating the symptoms and are unwilling to look deeper within for the actual source of what's going on, then we're missing some wonderful opportunities. We are also most likely making our life more challenging than it has to be.

Those challenges can present in many ways in our life and work. But they will always create some level of resistance, like feeling overscheduled, etc., etc. In Buddha's *Four Noble Truths,* the first of the four is acknowledging that there is a challenge or issue in our life. Having worked with thousands of people through the years, I can tell you that this first truth is one of the hardest for most people.

If we are paying enough attention and are being mindful of our feelings and needs, we'll be able to acknowledge when our shell starts to feel a little snug. This awareness and acknowledgement gives us the opportunity to take action on the second truth, which is looking more deeply within for the origin of what is causing us to get off track. By being willing to go more deeply within and find the source of an issue, we can then apply the third truth and stop doing whatever it is that is causing the issue. In stopping the cause, we can then apply the fourth truth, which is to start living more consciously from a higher perspective, beyond those challenges we've now resolved. We can then see that healing is possible, which gives us hope.

The fourth noble truth is also about choosing a life path that supports us in applying the first three truths whenever something comes up. The fourth step is made up of what Buddha calls *The Noble Eightfold Path.* We can just call it living a conscious and mindful life. No, you don't have to become a Buddhist, you just get to benefit now from the wisdom of the past.

Challenges are the opportunities in our life to grow. The extent of your resistance to any change, reflects the magnitude of the change you are being called to. If you don't want to engage in a tug-of-war, then drop your end of the rope. Living in the present allows you to notice the tugging and mindfully let go. This is how it all works. With your higher intention to serve and support others, you don't have to focus on the money or all of the "hows." You know that. We only need to learn to trust and be present, making sure that each step we take is leading us in the direction of our highest intention, so we can fulfill our greatest potential.

The cost of not going within:

Please keep in mind that, regardless of whether you see what's going on in your life as a limitation, an issue, a problem, or a challenge, what is truly going on is that you are being called up to another level. Any signs of discord are only due to the level of resistance that you, either consciously or unconsciously, are having with the transformation. There's nothing to worry about – it's just time for a larger shell. Yippee!

We touched on the costs of the lobster not changing his shell, and while death seems a bit overstated for our unwillingness to let go and transform, it's actually not. As Neale Donald Walsh said, "Life begins outside of your comfort zone." A question that I have asked people over the years is, "What percentage of your energy do you use to keep your emotional backlog stuffed safely down within your gut?" In the context of when I ask the question, they always know the answer, and the answer is often at least 40% or even much more.

As clients and I look at this together, they begin to realize just how hard they are pushing down on that brake pedal of life. They also begin to see how much it's costing them in all aspects of their life. The reasons they are investing so much of their energy into keeping that backlog under control generally come down to, "If I ever let it out, then nobody would love me; I'd be all alone. I'm afraid that I'd be alone and die." In other words, they believe that their very survival depends on their keeping that emotional backlog in check. And as you'll see in chapter five, there are some very real reasons that they feel this way.

Keep in mind that when I talk about someone's level of personal power, I'm also talking about the degree to which they are able to open their heart and love, their level of consciousness, how confident and joyful they feel, and so on and so forth. In other words, what keeps people stuck with their foot on the brake is a deep-seated belief that if they are fully in their power and unconditionally loving themselves, they will be all alone and worse. And the bigger truth is that their fear of this social or literal death results in a fear of life and living fully.

We'll get into the depths of all this in the following chapters. For now, though, let's just say that keeping our foot on the brake and resisting our natural evolution, can and does result in the dramas and difficulties of life. Sometimes it affects our health, sometimes our relationships. For others, it may show up as financial struggles, or spiritual crises. For still others, it results in never understanding their purpose or never really feeling passionate about life. They may never feel quite connected, authentic, complete, or enough. For you, keeping your foot on the brake, however lightly, may just be keeping you out of the flow that you're looking for, and preventing you from being able to take your life and work up to the next level.

Let's just say that the cost is far too high. The only result that can and ever does happen, when someone heals their emotional backlog, is that they more fully accept and love themself. This self-love and acceptance are then, of course, reflected throughout their entire life. That I can guarantee. Perhaps it helps to appreciate that to the degree that we have our foot on the brake, is the same degree to which we keep our heart from fully opening.

Sleuthing the source:

When someone approaches me with a symptom or a known or unknown deeper challenge, I go through the same process of elimination that I'd go through when facing any challenge. For example, years ago, I created a lovely water feature in the back corner of our yard. There is a stream that wends its way down the hillside, gently tumbling over falls and rapids, and then flows into a large, organically-shaped pond.

I built in all of the filtration, UV lights, and whatnots it needs to keep the water clear and lovely. This serene setting has been one of those little joys in my life. After about 15 years, the water started getting more algae in it and wasn't clearing up. I first fiddled with and fixed the UV lights, but nothing changed. Then I added a couple of supposedly magic bullets, bacteria-based solutions, but nothing changed. Then I had my gardener take apart and clean up the two filters and make sure they were working, and nothing happened. I changed out the water, but, within a few days it was back to nasty again.

I finally surrendered and called a water feature expert. He, of course, walked me through his logical checklist to see what the cause may be. Being "the kind of guy who can build a shopping mall with a Q-tip and a pocket knife" (Anne Heche from the 1998 movie *Six Days Seven Nights*), I was pleased to say yes to his long list of questions. That is, until the last couple of suggestions, where he was recommending steps that I hadn't considered or known to take. His suggestions, of course, worked, and we were back to enjoying our lovely stream and pond again.

The truth is that I'm pretty much an expert in water features from my work as a designer and builder of Japanese gardens. I even wrote a chapter for Sunset Books on designing and constructing waterfalls, streams, and ponds. But when I got stuck, it was great to consult someone with the expertise and a different perspective, so that we could work together and handle the challenge. We even enjoyed the process.

Yes, this is relevant to your challenge, so please stay with me for a moment. When clients come to me with a challenge, I go through the questions that logically take us through the elimination process of what they have handled and what might not have been considered. Keep in mind that more than a few of the clients that come to me are experts in their fields, and our fields often times overlap. But, by asking the right questions about five key areas of their life's journey, and logically looking for what they haven't handled, we are always able to get to the deeper source of their challenge. Knowing the source then allows us to identify the cause and what they need to shift in order to resolve the issue. My clients also, of course, come away from our work with a bigger perspective of life, so they don't run into this issue again.

What I'd like to share with you is an overview of the five crucial steps needed to resolve your challenges and enhance your life. Once you have initially taken and become more and more familiar with these five steps, they will continue to benefit you for a lifetime. You will find that you more easily see a challenge or growth opportunity and know how to go deep within to find out what the source of any issue is. Once you have acknowledged the challenge and found the source, then it is easier to know how to resolve and heal that deeper cause. The real bonus is that each time you do this five-step process, you will also have greater clarity as to how you can and probably want to create your life. This allows you to keep the dramas and challenges to a minimum, so that your chosen life unfolds more smoothly.

While there is so much more to each of these steps that you'll find incredibly useful on your entire life's journey, I'll just briefly introduce them here and give you a sense of how they are completely interrelated. For example, in step one, to be able to change your core program you'll need to breathe (step two) and rewire your brain (step three). Breathing is a key aspect of all of the steps and to be able to fully integrate your whole brain in step three you will have had to change your core programming. It is necessary to have done all three of these steps to be able to fully enjoy steps four (mindfulness) and five (accessing Big Mind). Having gone through all five steps, you'll find that they then each support and enhance the others.

Overview of the 5 Steps of Personal Evolution:

Step One is about recognizing your core programming that you first began developing in earliest childhood. We'll explore how and why that core programming is relevant to you today, and even its relationship to your being overscheduled. We'll look at how your early programming is working for you now, and how it can be upgraded to better serve you on this higher level of play.

In Step Two, we'll explore how to use your breathing as a gauge that lets you be aware of even the subtlest indications that a challenge or growth opportunity is arising. This allows you to more proactively move into creating your life. You will also understand the many ways you can use your breath to journey into the depths of your inner cave to identify what is going on and how best to resolve it.

We'll also explore how you can use different breathing patterns that allow you to literally choose your level of consciousness and have the awareness to keep in touch with what you are feeling and needing. Using the breath to quiet the mind allows you access to your whole, integrated brain, and even Big Mind – both of which we'll examine in the following steps.

In Step Three, we'll explore how to fully access and integrate your whole brain. This opens you up to developing revolutionary ways of thinking and being. Here you'll learn to live from those enticing places you have perhaps only felt when you've been in the zone. Learn how to think in an all-encompassing way, similar to that of Michelangelo, and explore even higher states of being, living, and creativity. As you breathe and learn to quiet the brain, you will discover how to access Big Mind and levels of creativity and insight you have only perhaps touched on before.

Step Four introduces you to and gives you a lifetime pass into meta-mindfulness. Meta-mindfulness, to me, is a wholly-inclusive form of mindfulness – one in which you are aware of everything from a higher, yet still very focused, integrated perspective. This is in contrast to the type of mindfulness where you pay attention only to one, isolated thing, to the exclusion of everything else. Meta-mindfulness allows you to be like the Bobby Fisher of mindfulness. In this level of presence, you will slow down time and be able to create your dreams from your highest state of consciousness. This isn't just telling you what you already know about being mindful; it's showing you how to take it deeper and how to fully integrate and live from that inclusive, present, mindful state. These first four steps are about living and working in the world at a very high level of functioning.

Step Five is about gaining access to Big Mind. Big Mind is that level of consciousness that pervades all of existence – the level of consciousness where universal intelligence resides. When you access Big Mind, you can receive any insights or information you need from the Universal Library at will. The first four steps also set the stage for the quantum fifth step, where you access Big Mind, which is that bridge on the edge of silence where you can receive from the infinite. It is that unique space where you are both the wave and the ocean. As the wave, you are able to access and draw on the wisdom and awareness of that ocean. You discover how to, at any time and for as long as you want, be in and create from that place. Talk about an amazing way to resolve your worldly challenges and take your work and life up to the next level – this is it!

How it all fits together:

You will be using various breathing processes to gain greater access to the deeper regions within, so that you can better understand and appreciate your initial core programming. As you learn how to rewrite that old, unsupportive programming, you will find that your mind becomes quieter.

Your quieter mind makes it easier for you to connect the various areas of your brain, so that they can work together as a unified team. You will be able to breathe into a quieter place and, from there, more consciously begin to eliminate unsupportive neuronal patterns that have fired and wired together throughout much of your life. You will also be able to more consciously initiate the development of new and more supportive neuronal pathways.

As you begin to relax and breathe – relax and trust – your mind and body begin to work together. The chemical gates within your brain open up and connect and integrate even more fully. You find yourself relaxing, trusting, breathing, and being more creative, intuitive, and literally smarter than you were before.

You'll find that you feel more confident and can concentrate more deeply. With a bigger picture perspective, you see the optimal paths and choices for your life. Your enhanced ability to focus and be mindful will allow you to get more done more easily and with greater quality than ever before. When you find yourself dealing with a question or challenging situation, you'll know how to breathe and quiet your mind to a depth where you can access Big Mind. With that enhanced connection, you will receive the insight, information, or guidance that best serves you and everyone involved.

Yes, life will still have many challenges, but now you'll see each of those challenges as another gift, an opportunity to develop and grow along your life's path. Sure, you might still forget from time to time, but you'll now have what you need to remember and get back on track. Your highest intention in life becomes your guiding light. Life's choices become simplified: If any given option supports your higher intention, you go for it; if it doesn't, then you let it go.

You no longer find yourself overscheduled by success or neglecting to nurture your most important relationships. You'll take better care of yourself, too. And, if you notice you're not, then it's another opportunity to grow through the five steps again. Each time you do this, it will become easier and a more natural part of your life. While initially the steps may take months, in time and with practice, it may only take a breath.

A spiritual teacher of mine once shared that being on the path is like being a piece of wood that is being gently sanded down. The knots are the hardest areas and can take a while to smooth out, but over time, breath by breath, meditation by meditation, life challenge by life challenge, we get smoother and smoother.

As you well know, the cost of not doing this work is that the knots continue to stick out and snag on whatever is coming into our life. We tend to bump into, rather than flow around, the river rocks of life. We get attached to looking and being who we are, (and possibly who others expect us to be), and so every change is a threat to that comfort zone we've grown to identify as our life. The stream isn't all that gentle, and it can sometimes feel like we're struggling to row upstream rather than rowing gently down the stream.

And as you also know, there are infinite degrees of ease and struggle, resistance and flow. I imagine that you look around and reasonably feel that you're doing a great job with your work and your life. And I'd agree – you are. The question, though, that's always there for us, is: "What level do you want to play on?" Have you done so well that you are going to start ignoring your life's indicators that it's time to grow a larger shell?

Perhaps, in your case, you just want the outer hassles and symptoms to go away, so you can get on with your work. But isn't there a little part of you that really would like to breathe a little deeper, heal a bit more fully, and take it all up to another level of consciousness? You know that there really isn't anything that's outside of yourself that is overscheduling you. You know that it's not ultimately the busyness of your success that is keeping you from taking better care of yourself and opening up to a deeper and more connected relationship. I know you know that it really is your choice as to what level you want to play on.

When my exclusive clients come to me to break free of their little nudging niggles or major life-quakes, my main job is to confidentially serve and support them through these 5 Steps of Personal Evolution. As it always happens, it's those inner shifts that end the outer struggle and bring about the richer life expansion they've been looking for all along.

Chapter 4

Step 1: Upgrade Your Core Programming

"You will not be punished for your anger, you will be punished by your anger."
—Buddha

As you well know, we humans come into this world almost helpless. I've watched a newborn colt stand up and run within an hour of birth. We've all watched the nature programs where baby turtles, just moments after breaking free of their leathery shell, scurry in a mad dash for the sea in a race for their life. Baby humans, on the other hand (that's you and me), can't even roll over. We are born so utterly helpless that without the care of someone else, we'd surely die.

But, the key word in that opening sentence turns out to be "almost." We do have one instinctual skill, and that is making a connection with a caretaker. Our cry can open up their hearts, and our facial expressions can make them empathize with and want to care for us. We instinctually know that without them, we won't make it. So, in our early beginnings, connecting with caretakers becomes our primary focus and is literally a matter of life or death.

During our first few weeks and months of life, we learn which sounds will get our desired response. We notice what facial expressions draw someone in enough to connect and take care of us. We know that the most important thing is to get that connection, and the deeper that connection is, the safer we are and the more likely we will survive. This is really an inborn part of our human primal behavior. While we'll take any support we can get, what we really want is someone who is dedicated to our needs and who cares that we're doing well. Later we will learn to call that connection "love." In the meantime, we do our very best to figure out what it is we need to do and who we need to be to get as much of that care and connection as we can.

So, there we are, within months of being born, coming up with the most effective program we can to get as much love as we can in our unique situation. I've asked thousands of people around the world what a child wants more than anything else, and sure enough, the immediate and confident answer is always "Love."

The next question I ask is, "So if a child wants love more than anything else, then what are they willing to do to get it?" Again, the consistent response is always some form of "Whatever it takes." So, with all of the research I've read and the thousands of people I've worked with saying the same thing, I'm going to trust that "love" really is what a child wants more than anything else. It also is abundantly clear that, as a child, we will indeed do just about anything we can to make sure we get as much of it as we can.

The next question I ask is, "As a child, what kind of love do we want?" There's the conditional "I'll love you if…" kind of love, and then there's the unconditional "I'll love you no matter what" kind of love. You can probably guess the answer to this one, too. So, if, as a child, you wanted unconditional love more than anything else, the next logical question is, "What were you willing to do to get it?" In other words, what strategy did you come up with to optimize the amount of attention and love that you could get in your particular situation within your unique family dynamics?

If you take a good look back on your own childhood, I trust that, like thousands of others before you, you'll be able to come up with your specific answer to that question. Some people say they were good or quiet. Others felt like they needed to perform or achieve. When I was growing up, there were very clear expectations for what a boy should be like and how a girl should behave in order to be accepted by their family and society. Today those rules are changing, but trust me, there are still plenty of images, expectations, and rules that others will want you to follow. Each of us finds our way and the primary focus of that way (consciously or not) is generally, even as we get older, how we can get the most acceptance and love from others in our unique situation.

No, most of us didn't get the amount of love or the unconditional love that we truly wanted, but, if we survived, then we at least got enough love to get us into adulthood. So, what was your program for optimizing the amount of love that you could get from your mom and family? Did you look around at how your parents got love from each other, or how siblings were getting love, and come up with your own unique program? What was the niche that worked for you?

It's not uncommon for the oldest, for example, to take on a role similar to the dominant parent, or for the middle child to try to keep everybody happy and getting along. If there was a third child, they see that those other strategies are taken and they might just be more laid back and interested in having fun. Sometimes being bad was the only way that a child got attention. The attention they received might have been in the form of punishment, but at least they were getting some recognition.

My core program was a bit of a mix as, on the one hand, I tried to do everything perfectly so my dad would love me, and on the other hand, I'd be a little obnoxious and funny to entertain my mom and older sister. Again, just play along and consider what your program was, and perhaps what your parents' and sibling's programs were for getting love. My mom's, for example was, to always give more than she got; Dad worked hard and liked to joke around. It all seemed to work out pretty well.

Whatever that early childhood program was that you developed, it was probably perfect for your unique circumstance. I'm always amazed and impressed how, with every client who shares their story, they were intuitive and aware enough at a very young age to get as much of that love as they could in their unique family circumstances. For some it was easier, while for others, it was a struggle for survival.

Yes, we all wanted more – more love, attention, recognition, ease – but congratulations on doing such an amazing job. How do I know I can congratulate you? Well, because you are here, reading or listening to this sentence. If you hadn't done such a great job, you'd either not have made it or you'd be in such bad shape physically, emotionally, or otherwise, that we wouldn't be having this conversation. So again, nice going!

I imagine by now you're wondering what this core program for getting love could possibly have to do with your current challenges that come from being so successful. The answer is, *everything*. As you developed that early program, you decided how confident you could be, how much being in your power worked with others, and even how much you could accept and love yourself. I venture to say that your early program for getting love directly influences the way you show up in your life today, which, in turn, determines the specific challenges you are likely experiencing.

As you moved through the months and the years of your life, you were almost constantly focused on what was going on outside of yourself, so you could figure out how to fit in and get along with others. You were looking at and exploring who and what you could be. You were also looking for what was okay to emotionally feel and express, and which emotions needed to be ignored and suppressed. You determined what was acceptable in your world and what wasn't; who was acceptable and who wasn't. Fitting in meant connection, connection meant love, and love meant survival.

This was all good. This was all perfect and exactly what you needed to do and should have been doing. The problem is, that over the years, we've made a really big investment in that program for getting acceptance and love. Over time, most of us generally get very attached, albeit unconsciously, to our program for getting love. We become so adept at and protective of our winning strategy, that it becomes an inherent part of our comfort zone and how we move through the world. While deep down we still long for that elusive unconditional love we always wanted as a child, as we mature, we are practical enough to just accept whatever love we can get.

And while that program we developed was perfect for our early years and most likely did optimize the amount of love you were able to receive in your family, you might find that it is now limiting your success out in the world with others. Maybe your program is still getting you love, but it may be coming with a lot of other costs and compromises that you really don't like, maybe don't recognize, or don't even necessarily know how to deal with.

The real problem is that as you move into adulthood, your strong tendency is often to still rely on that old childhood program for getting love. You are still looking outside of yourself to figure out who and what you should be. Like most of us, you will tend to be playing within the limitations that others are giving you.

I've had thousands of clients do a sentence completion exercise where they start with looking at, "If I love myself unconditionally, I'm afraid that..." and we take that breath by breath, deeper and deeper until the sentence is inevitably completed with something like "...others won't like me." It gets even more interesting as we go even deeper still, but for now the point is that deep down, people feel that unconditionally accepting and loving themselves will result in somehow being rejected by others. Yes, there was the Christ thing and the Martin Luther King thing, that may support that fear, but let's explore this a bit more.

No, I'm not guiding my clients into saying anything in particular. Not doing that is a part of the art of my work. Where they get to is just a deep-seated fear that it turns out nearly everybody has, and which unfortunately ends up sabotaging our acceptance and deeper levels of love for ourselves. The same fear surfaces with the sentence completion of, "If I'm in my power..." and several other similar revealing sentences.

It turns out that the success we had with that early program for getting love has us later in life still looking outside of ourselves for the unconditional love that we need to first find within. That old program that was so great for us as a child, can totally limit and suck for us as an adult.

To start with, regardless of what our specific program was, we become conditioned and even addicted to looking outside of ourselves for all of the answers that we can only find within. To a very costly degree, we give up our power. Most of us also fail to fully see or embrace our deeper purpose and passion, just so that we can fit in. Our relationships are never quite as satisfying as we'd like, because that person isn't giving us the unconditional love that we really want from them. We end up always wanting more than they are able to give us. The problem, of course, is that if we don't unconditionally love and accept ourselves, our inner relationships are simply mirrored in our outer relationships with others. Keep in mind, I didn't make up the rules here, I'm just trying to help you better appreciate and understand the game. As you well know, when we're dealing with something in our life, regardless of what it is, a new and bigger perspective can make all the difference.

As a successful leader, you have, no doubt, handled many personal growth and career challenges in order to get you to where you are in life. Without question, you most likely have a great collection of tools and processes you've developed and may even be teaching to others. I trust that you have been regularly using those tools and techniques to deal with your current challenges, yet they may not be creating the results that you are looking for. If you're up against something that your tried and true methods aren't taking care of, you may be feeling kind of stuck.

Let's take another look at the childhood programming we're talking about. I appreciate that you might want to take a deep breath and, in exasperation, tell me how you have already done that work before. You have done this or that program, worked on this or that family issue, gotten in touch with your inner child or whatever it is that you have done. I get it. I really do.

I want you to know that I recognize the amazing amount of work you've done on yourself. You couldn't be the successful leader that you are, had you not made that investment. I also understand that the way that you have done your life has brought you incredible success. I do see and absolutely appreciate that.

As a matter of fact, that is the very reason I'm writing this book to you. I see you and I value who you are and what you do so much, that I want to be there for you so that you can continue to grow, enjoy your life, and keep on helping tons more people create their most fulfilling lives as well. I remember years ago hearing about a swing coach that Tiger Woods enlisted. My first thought was, "Tiger's the best, who in the world could help him?" Then I realized that that is exactly what I do in a different realm.

The irony is that I had forgotten that one of my clients was the tennis coach for one of the top tennis players in the world. So even the top players need coaches and even those coaches need coaches. All of our issues and challenges are created in relationship to other people, and they, of course, need to be dealt with and resolved in relationship with other people.

I remember working in a small group with a Shaman friend of mine. We were a few hours into the process, and my stomach started to feel like it was tying itself into all of the many knots that I'd learned for sailing. While screaming came up for me as one option, I decided to first try breathing and letting go more. Nothing changed. In frustration, I opened my arms out wide to either side, and in doing so accidently touched the arm of the person next to me. That little momentary touch released all of that tension and pain that I was going through. It reminded me – again – how critically important connecting with others is to our releasing and healing process.

The first step, and often times one of the most difficult in handling and growing from a challenge in our life, is to acknowledge that we are dealing with something that is disturbing our life. The longer we take to acknowledge and recognize something's not how we'd like it to be, the more disruptive and even dramatic that challenge will become. The sooner we recognize a disturbance "in the Force," the sooner we can embrace the change we are in and the easier it will be to take the steps to turn a struggle or challenge into an opportunity. Yes, I know that you know that too, but sometimes it's helpful to be reminded.

So, with all of that said, all I'm suggesting is that I trust you have been and are doing your best. Nice going! But if you're not getting the results you want, then you might want to consider either looking at a couple of new tools, or going in a little deeper, and seeing what's stuck and keeping you from expanding further out. You may wish to breathe into a more mindful place where you can better see the problem, solution, and potential results – where you can access a more integrated, whole brain approach to the challenge, and get help from what I'd call "Big Mind" or Higher-Self. Just saying....

Perhaps you have learned on your journey that your true power lies in letting go. You may have also recognized that whatever is challenging you in your life is a gift that you could actually enjoy opening. If you appreciate this may be the case, then let's continue with our chat.

Growing up in the Northwest, from very early childhood I was off every day exploring the woods, nearby lakes, and Puget Sound. As a champion rower and then a Marine, I had learned that life was like a chess game and you had to plan many moves ahead. I felt that developing a certain level of toughness was part of growing up. It wasn't until after some very brutal lessons in my twenties that I came to realize that my real strength was in being vulnerable. That shift of shedding my previously honed shell took years of exploration and doing what used to be called "the work."

I will always remember and be forever grateful to John Gray and Barbara DeAngelis for the start into emotional healing that their work gave me. The Zen spiritual community I belonged to at the time had a clear undertone that emotions were just something to be ignored and denied. John and Barbara's early work together helped me to start recognizing my feelings and understanding how critically important it was to not only acknowledge my feelings, but to also fully express and release them. Instead of being about toughening up, my journey became one of softening and becoming more vulnerable as I learned to open up my heart. It turned out to be a life-saving and life-enhancing change of direction.

Having looked at and healed my past was one of the most empowering aspects of my journey, so I was amazed when certain well-respected transformational leaders started telling people to just ignore the past. Various leaders wrote books about just being happy for no reason, ignoring the deeper inner reasons we may not be at peace within. Many also built their teaching platforms upon head-in-the-sand perspectives such as, "the past belongs in the past and has no place in the present." They came up with all sorts of quick fixes and distractive processes for looking outside of ourselves at how to gloss over and ignore the past. Over time, of course, I witnessed how these leaders and their communities continued to ignore, yet be very much at the effect of, limitations stemming from their past.

While the Buddha did say "Do not pursue the past." it is only by taking this quote completely out of context that anyone could possibly consider that he was saying that the past has absolutely no connection with or deep influence on our life in the present. Thich Nhat Hahn explains that Buddha was merely saying that we shouldn't allow ourselves to be overwhelmed by our past. He wasn't saying that we should stop looking at our past, but rather that we should observe it deeply.

While the proof of this is seen throughout Buddha's sutras or talks, we see repeatedly in the sutra on the Four Establishments of Mindfulness where he encourages the audience to not repress fear, anger, or unpleasant feelings. Rather than ignore our past, he emphatically teaches us how to breathe into these feelings, knowing that they are the source of many of our psychological and physiological problems, and our inability to be present.

Thich Nhat Hahn says, "To repress our feelings is to repress ourselves." It is only by breathing into, mindfully observing, and transforming these feelings that we can heal them, so we are no longer at the effect of them. To the degree that we heal our past is the degree to which we are able to create a clear and compelling present – both for ourselves and for the world.

Yes, I appreciate that if a leader hasn't done that deeper work, they will likely encourage others to ignore it also. But I also appreciate the tremendous cost to those trusting followers who have been so significantly misled.

I can only imagine that you too have gone through some very difficult challenges that have ended up teaching you some of your most valuable lessons.

In addition to the enhanced perspectives I've received from Buddha's teachings, Thich Nhat Hahn's interpretations, and guidance from my various wise mentors, Joseph Campbell, my earliest mentor, also opened me up to new perspectives and empowering insights. We had invited him to come give a talk at a college I taught at, and I had the privilege of driving him around and having a memorably long lunch with him overlooking the beach. Through the years, we got to know each other better as we walked the woods of Big Sur. He wanted to know more about meditation, and I was awed by his stories of The Hero's Journey. The gifts Joe shared with me continue to influence my work and enhance my life's story.

As I am sure you have also learned on your path, The Hero's Journey is not a one-and-done experience but an ongoing process that repeatedly cycles through our life. Our inner cave isn't just something we explore one time to grab all the treasures we can hold, but a sacred place to which we return again and again. Each time we go a little deeper within so that we can expand out into our life and the world. While initially that inner cave was a terrifying place for me to go, over time it has become a sanctuary where I know I can find the perfect awareness to take my life and contribution up to the next level.

I've had a growing insight about the Hero's Journey that I'd love to go back and be able to talk about with Joe. At this point in my life, it appears that there are really three notable phases of hero's journeys in our personal evolution. The first is taking a look at our past and seeing what we are at the effect of -- what limitations or unsupportive beliefs it is time for us to heal and change. For people on this first phase of the journey, their strength comes from remembering and accepting all of who and what they are.

Having healed the past, the second phase seems to be more about who we want to be and what we want to do. What is our purpose and passion and how do we want to participate and show up in the world? For people playing on this second level, their sense of power comes from their being and doing, and their accomplishments.

The third phase is for those who have mostly gone beyond their fears, desires, and images of who they are and what life should be like. People playing on this level have explored beyond the self and physical realms and are mindfully aware of the inter-relatedness of all of existence. Theirs is a journey of acceptance and surrendering. Their focus is more on being than doing, knowing that vulnerability is truly a source of strength. Of course, like all of life, the three phases are interrelated, and, as you know, there can be more than a few journeys within each phase.

I totally appreciate that you have handled many of your personal challenges in and through the work that you have done in your life. We're not here, having this little chat, to make you or your family of origin wrong. We're not here to discover any mistakes you may feel you've made in the past. I trust, as I imagine you do, that your journey has given you exactly what it was that you needed, so that you could remember and grow into being the amazing, successful person you are.

What we are doing here is recognizing that you're bumping up against something. There are some clear indicators in your life that something is going on that makes you feel like you're struggling or having to deal with something that's throwing you off a bit. The truth is, what I'd honestly like to say is, "Congratulations!" It's important for you to remember that it's only because you've been moving forward on your path that you are bumping into anything. It's because you have been asking more of life, and that disturbance in the "Force" you're experiencing is an indicator that you are now ready to shift and play on a higher level.

Many transformational leaders share how thoughts create reality. While this is true, what they don't show you is how to go to the source of those subconscious and unsupportive thoughts and completely change your old programming that keeps you repetitively creating your old, unsupportive reality. Once that old core program is upgraded, you will find that supportive new thoughts and behaviors naturally evolve. The following three pieces constitute the very foundation of your personal evolution.

Healing your emotional backlog:

By my mid-twenties, I'd been meditating for a few years with some relative success of quieting my thoughts. Of all of the techniques I'd learned, using the breath was by far my best guide. I started to recognize that most of my thoughts were about the past and the future, and that I had a lot of images and expectations about myself, others, and about the world. As I breathed more deeply into the noise, I could feel how much various fears and desires around these images and expectations made up most of the thoughts that distracted me during meditation and throughout my life. As I watched my monkey-mind, it was easy to see that most of it was just noise. Rather than helping me or solving any problems, it became clear that my busy mind was distracting me from being the focused, powerful, peaceful, and accomplished leader that I felt life was offering me.

During my work with John and Barbara, I saw how important it was to acknowledge and express my emotions, but I later saw how important it was to also release those emotions and move on from those early core stories. As I healed my emotional backlog, I noticed my mind getting quieter. As I pieced together that my emotional backlog was primarily the source for my monkey mind, I began to look even deeper at the origin of my stuffed-down emotions.

Recognizing that attention and love were what we wanted most as a child, I realized that it was around that core programming that most, if not all, of my emotional backlog had developed. Since I was a child, I had been looking outside of myself to others for love and acceptance. Now as an adult, who had healed and moved beyond that old program, it was time to write a new program for getting love. And it had to start with unconditionally accepting and loving myself.

The more I healed and moved beyond being at the effect of the past, the quieter my mind became. The more I healed my childhood program for getting love, the less drama and more presence I felt in my life. As I developed exercises and programs that supported my clients in healing their old love programs, they shared how much quieter their minds were becoming too. I also watched them develop an interest in meditation, and from there, they'd naturally expand the vision for their lives.

Based on results, my clients, meditation students, and I discovered together that the best way to quiet our minds in meditation was to do the healing work of going back and re-parenting and healing our inner child. Step one in the path of an empowering personal journey was set.

A quiet mind, as it turns out, is a spacious and uncluttered mind. It supports laser focus and clarity of purpose. It also creates an interesting paradox with time. As the chatter in the mind slows, time seems to expand. It's almost like being able to create time, as you more effectively and efficiently use the time you have. When you combine quieting the mind with releasing subconscious limitation and inner sabotage, the difference feels like that between driving on an unpaved bumpy road in an old jalopy, versus cruising the autobahn in a high-performance BMW.

As newer clients came to understand all of this, I'd ask them what percentage of their energy they'd estimate they were using to make sure that their stuffed-down emotions stayed deeply hidden. Sometimes reluctantly, but more often in tears, they recognized that they had been wasting probably half of their energy in holding back and keeping emotions stuffed down. As they would heal their emotional backlog, it was like watching them take their foot off the brake and recognize just how amazingly powerful they truly are. The energy that they had been using to keep their emotional backlog denied and safely stored away was now available for them to use in creating their next dream. And with their foot off the brake pedal and now on the gas, combined with clarity about where they were headed and why, they met their goals infinitely faster, with quite a bit more joy and ease.

Of course, we also discovered why the onion analogy is so appropriate for our healing process. As we remove each of the outer layers, we reveal more of our true essence. The great news was that even though that deep work seemed scary as hell in the beginning, it not only got easier, but more exciting. Many of us on the path began to appreciate that each layer we moved into gave us another opportunity to remember, heal, and reintegrate another aspect of ourselves into our lives.

All of those parts of our life that we had shoved down and tried to ignore, because they didn't fit into what we felt was acceptable to others, were now being invited back in. We came to realize that they were all crucial parts of who and what we are. We needed all of those disparate parts so that we could remember, accept, and love the entirety of who we are. We needed all those parts of us so that we could become an integrated, whole being again.

While you may have done a lot of great work, and have little flotsam and jetsam from your past that could rise to the surface, it's still worth exploring and clearing up whatever arises. Every person I've worked with has found this inner exploration to be a wise investment that pays life-long dividends.

While I used to take hours getting in and exploring my inner cave, now, when something comes up, I can just use my breath to go in and find out what's going on. Having learned to trust that whatever I find in there is a gift, I readily welcome whatever comes forward and stay more present with my life. Change is the one constant, and change facilitates our transformation. Change is good. I have come to trust that everything that comes into my life is a perfectly designed gift to help me even further open up my heart and love more fully. The universe is truly abundant and amazingly quite perfect.

Rewriting your program for getting love:

So how do you get to that place of trusting and welcoming change? And what does it take to be able to quiet your mind, slow down time, and expand your ability to create? To get to that level of flow in your life, you must first remove the blockages. We just talked about releasing and healing your emotional backlog in the section above, and that's a really good start. Now let's look at what's creating the noise and distraction on the inside. This is really the linchpin of everything that isn't working for you. When you address and clear this much less obvious blockage from within, you'll be amazed at how your time and creativity is freed up, your focus is sharpened, and your higher abilities become accessible to you. This is an essential piece of the puzzle, but probably not at all what you were expecting. Stay with me here, as this piece is a real life-changer.

As you resolve the source of your various distractions, your mind gets quiet and you're then able to accelerate and enhance your ability to create.

At the center of your core programming is your program for getting love. You have to release as much of the emotional backlog as you can around your old program for getting love. It is that emotional backlog that holds you to that habit of looking outside yourself for love, approval, and acceptance. In order to break free from your old, often unconscious limitations (like those "not enough" beliefs or "I need to say yes to others whenever possible,"), it's super important to rewrite your program for getting love to one where you're looking within rather than outside yourself for love, approval, and acceptance.

So, the key question I'd like you to seriously consider is, *"What was your program for getting love?"* Or put another way: What was the program you created as a young child, that optimized the amount of acceptance and love you could get in your family? While most people would rather avoid looking at this question, the reason I ask is that our early program for getting love is often directly connected to the challenges we are experiencing in our life today. Yes, I recognize that your challenges might seem unrelated. In fact, they're probably presenting as normal problems such as being overscheduled, not taking great care of yourself, relationship issues, or running into resistance or difficulties in getting to those goals that are really important to us.

Being aware of your early program for getting love is one of the most important things that you can know, as it had a huge influence on who and what you became as you grew up. It was this program that had you looking outside of yourself to figure out what was acceptable to feel and express and what needed to be stuffed down. It was this program that defined how big or how small you were willing to play in life. It colored all of your perspectives and experience as you were growing up. It was this program that taught you to initially look outside of yourself for what you would later realize could only be found within.

For years, there have been many thought leaders who have unknowingly misguided us with declarations that "The past is the past. It has no effect or influence on the present and is best just left alone." Well, I'm here to tell you, that couldn't be further from the truth! Even the mainstream medical establishment is now finally acknowledging that early life experiences matter, and that "We all shape our reality around a story that we have internalized about the world and our role in it."

And while it is true that we can't change what happened, we can go back in and change the meaning we attributed to past events and the decisions and definitions we made about ourselves as a result. We can also go back in and rewrite that core program that has us looking outside ourselves for love, acceptance, and approval. Our original program for getting love is actually what most often derails us in our life. Don't get me wrong, that early program you created by two or three years old was an absolutely brilliant strategy for maximizing the amount of love you received from your parents or caregivers. But what was brilliant in that context becomes limiting when that same basic strategy is played out now, as an adult. For example, let's say that, when you were a young child, you got the most love and approval from Mom and Dad when you were agreeable. You learned early on that saying "Yes" and doing what your parents asked you to do got you the most praise, hugs, rewards, and serenity in the home. Good strategy!

But here you are, many decades later, and you may find yourself saying "Yes" more often than really works for you. "What could it hurt?" you might rationalize. You do a little benefit training here, a book review there, accept an impromptu dinner invitation, or say yes to delivering a keynote speech as a favor to an old friend and colleague. After all, you're quite capable at all of these things, and it makes those you're saying "Yes" to very happy. But your schedule becomes cramped and so do your life, health, relationships, and happiness. So that old program of "in order to get love, I need to do what others want me to do" is really counterproductive now. And for many people, they don't even recognize that they are still at the effect of that old unconscious programming from early childhood. We just see the end result which is, "My team keeps overscheduling me and I don't have time to take care of myself and work on my special projects."

To the degree that we supportively rewrite our program for getting love and have actually gone in and recovered, accepted, and healed the various parts of ourselves, is the degree to which that change will be reflected in the alignment of our thoughts, emotions, and our ability to fulfill our highest intentions. This is our power, our love, and our awareness in action. As we awaken and reintegrate those parts of ourselves that were once tucked away, hidden, or denied for the sake of getting acceptance and love from others, we also awaken our spirit and begin to access all that we need to live a genuinely happy, successful life. Any misalignment that we recognize in our outer life, (such as being overscheduled) often includes a disconnection within ourselves that can be supportively made whole again.

Looking outside of ourselves has us trying to identify who or what to blame for circumstances in our life. Looking outside for what is okay for us to feel, be, or do results in our giving up our power to someone else. I know that assertion feels like nails on a chalkboard to you, and I'm glad. I totally get it.

While looking for love outside of ourselves as a child was perfect and completely appropriate, as an adult it limits us to being what others expect or want us to be. The real kicker is that the love – and especially that unconditional love that we wanted more than anything as a child – is, at least unconsciously, still what we want the most as an adult. Look at how being overscheduled gives you an opportunity to examine how that old program or remnants of it may still be playing out in your life. Perhaps it's very little or seemingly insignificant. Perhaps it's enough to throw you off a bit and is worth handling.

The thing is that our outer relationships, especially the significant closer ones, are really just mirrors of our own inner relationship with ourselves. So, we generally can only let others love us to the degree that we accept and love ourselves. This, of course, gets played out in a lot of interesting ways. Everyone who comes into our life gives us the opportunity to see another part of ourselves. Our family, friends, people we work with, and our tribe all give us opportunities to reflect on and learn about who and what we are.

Here's a helpful little exercise for doing some inner mining of your own. Breathe and ask yourself the following questions: "What would it mean to you to solve this challenge? What, if any, benefits or upsides are there in your being overscheduled? What would be different in your life if you did resolve this challenge? If I weren't overscheduled I'm afraid that.... If I weren't overscheduled, I could...." Using these simple sentence completions can help you look within, into places and snags you might otherwise ignore. These inner places are only dark because we haven't yet brought them into the light. Perhaps the best time to do that is when they are jiggling around a bit and unsettling our life. Just perhaps.

The Big Game:

Another "blockage" that gets in the way of that quiet mind and expansive ability to create what you're looking for is something I call "The Big Game." This is another way we, often unconsciously, look outside ourselves for love, approval, and connection. By engaging in The Big Game, we inadvertently get in our own way and give up our power. And because we can't avoid or change the pitfalls we're not aware of, I thought it would be worthwhile to give this one a look.

The Big Game is something I discovered firsthand. It is a common and widely acceptable, yet largely unconscious, way we relate to and interact with one another. The Big Game is a social creation that has been maintained throughout millennia by people who have not done the work of going in to find out who and what they are.

As a young man, and as my childhood program for getting love matured beyond just my family, I learned that I was more accepted when I helped others. Over the years, I became highly skilled at making sure that others, and especially my girlfriends, felt great about themselves. I had watched how my dad had taken such great care of my mom, and how deeply they loved each other. So that strategy seemed like it would be a valuable part of my own approach for giving and getting love.

In my late twenties, I started to notice that I had a clear relationship pattern. Simplified, it came down to: Find a girl, rescue that girl, and then lose the girl. I began to see that, in order to play out my rescuer program, I needed to find a victim. Now, back in my day, a lot of girls had gotten love from their dad by acting helpless and girly. They had honed that skill so that Dad could rescue and show his love for them. This is, of course, quite unlike many of the empowered young women that I see today.

The only problem I had with my love strategy was that I was very good at actually rescuing the girls that I was involved with, and so within a year or two, they had stepped out of the victim role and into their power. The role of rescuer that I was playing to ensure their love for me wasn't alluring anymore. As I watched this play out in others' lives, I saw there were three main roles in what I came to call *The Big Game*. Why *The Big Game*? Because just about everybody was playing it.

The three main roles in *The Big Game* are now more commonly referred to as Rescuer, Victim, and Persecutor. The game is often played by couples, but even one person or several can participate. Generally, everyone has a favorite role, but people often switch roles, which keeps the game interesting. If, for example, there is a couple where one is primarily the victim and the other a rescuer, the victim (acting as a persecutor) could do something that upsets the rescuer (who then becomes the victim) and who then reacts (becoming the persecutor) by hurting the victim. This allows the person, who for a short time played the role of persecutor, to return to their more customary role as a victim. That, of course, triggers the rescuer to jump back into their preferred role as a rescuer. You can play with yourself, but two or more makes the game more interesting.

The idea is that as a rescuer I give love by offering to rescue. Of course, as a rescuer I need a victim, so the victim accepts my love and makes me feel valued and loved by setting up a partnership. Since we can always shift roles, the game stays interesting and filled with enough drama to hold our attention. The not so good news is that the quality of love you can get in this game, of looking for love and acceptance from outside of yourself, is far less satisfying than the unconditional kind of love that you really want – hence the 50% divorce rate in America.

As risky as it may seem, in order to share quality love with someone, you each need to love and accept yourself and be together because you want to be, not because you need to be. *The Big Game* relationship results in staying in a lower level, "I'll love you if...," conditional sort of love. By contrast, if you were to step out of *The Big Game* and do the work (that is, heal your emotional backlog and rewrite your program for getting love) then unconditional love is readily available to you, first from yourself, and then from others. When you are developing that unconditional love within and for yourself, you naturally attract people who are playing on that same level. This looks like two people who are on a marvelous adventure together, exploring ever-deeper connections within themselves, each other, and the world around them. They talk about those taboo topics that others are sure to avoid. That deeper trust creates a deeper understanding and appreciation of each other which results in greater trust, compassion, and even unconditional love – the very thing we've been looking for all along!

As a heart-centered, influential leader, it is, of course, imperative to "drive cleanly and responsibly." Not only does stepping out of The Big Game allow you to play and create on a higher level, but it also lets you model a happier, healthier way of being in the world. This piece fits right into your overall mission of making the world a better place.

To review, we step out of The Big Game by first healing our emotional backlog, which allows us to become quieter and more present. Next, we disengage from the game by rewriting our program for getting love, such that we stop looking for love, approval, and acceptance outside ourselves. Our new program goes something like, "In order to get love, I choose to love and accept myself unconditionally." As we put that new program into action, we begin to break the bonds of The Big Game's co-dependent interactions. There is no need to take on old roles or to play any games in order to interact and connect with others. We are whole and complete beings. We don't need anyone else to need us, to complete us, to approve of us, or to validate us. We do that all for ourselves. From this higher place of functioning, our interactions are clean, our boundaries are clear, we are being self-responsible, and that kind of connection is empowering for everyone. This is the communication style of an evolved influential leader – like you.

That was the case with Paul, whose story I shared with you in chapter one. He stopped taking on too many commitments, which was part of his old rescuer program. He had been unconsciously allowing his staff and even himself to overschedule him, because saying yes is how he used to get people to love him from his early childhood programming.

And what about those for whom their most common role was that of persecutor? Well, one client of mine who liked to rule with an iron fist found that by stepping out of The Big Game, he stopped losing clients and staff. He used to get so agitated around work that he wasted valuable time having to hire and retrain new staff and find new clients. Both clients and staff would leave pretty consistently because my client's vision of what it meant to be a strong businessman left them feeling either attacked, intimidated, or criticized. Before doing this work, he just thought that massive turnover was simply the nature of the beast. He'd never before considered that his early programming, his backlog of anger, abandonment issues, and mistrust, along with his preferred role of persecutor in The Big Game, had him acting like a beast. Turns out that his unconscious emotional backlog was exactly what was causing all the drama and upheaval that regularly went on in his business. "Pay attention or pay with pain," as one of the leaders I worked with used to say.

One of my female clients who unconsciously played The Big Game from "victim" as her go-to role, experienced a significant turn-around with these three pieces that make up the first step in my 5 Steps of Personal Evolution process. Once Grace did the inner work – releasing her emotional backlog and then learning how to be there for herself – she also stepped out of The Big Game. For the first time in her life (according to her), Grace stood firmly on her own two feet. She was still kind and gentle, as was her nature, but she learned to set clear and consistent boundaries and became a much more powerful leader in the process. Grace shared that she felt more grounded, much happier, and clear on her life's purpose. As she served from this newfound place of power and clarity, she also ended up quadrupling her income within a year. This work helped Grace put herself in the driver's seat – in charge of her time, her business interactions, and her life. Fortunately for us all, Grace has become a powerful mentor for young women on their path of healing.

Each of these leaders was having a challenge in their own way with time and staff, and not fully enjoying their work and the fruits of their success as much as they thought they would. They also felt too caught up in their own time constraints to step up and play the bigger game they had envisioned.

This work has proven time and again to be the way out. In this five-step process, each step builds upon the next, and it is absolutely necessary to have the clear and functional foundation in your life that this very first step offers. The other steps just can't work synergistically without this first one in place. You're in for a real treat, as this journey keeps getting a whole lot more interesting as you go!

Discovering the deeper source for the noise:

As a transformational therapist and an international meditation teacher, in my early thirties, I made it my quest to find out what was causing all the noise. Hundreds of people would come to hear me speak, filling hotel ballrooms, lecture halls, and castles around the planet. Each came with the same challenge – how to stop that all-too-familiar inner chatter from cluttering up their mind. With meditation being primarily about quieting the mind, I couldn't help but wonder why so many people were running around with a chattering monkey mind that they couldn't quiet down. Clearly, meditation alone was not the answer. As a therapist, I also pondered a similar question about what deeper source all of the issues, neuroses, and drama I saw my clients dealing with stemmed from. It turned out that the primary source for both was one and the same.

While these seemed like simple and logical questions, I had to go through a lot of reasonably good answers before I realized that most of those "solutions" focused on symptoms and not the deeper cause. As a doctor of chiropractic and a therapist, I fully realize that we are, as a society, addicted to just masking or doing our best to get rid of the symptoms of any challenges we run into – whether physical, emotional, mental, or social. But I also know that it is only by looking deeply enough for the root of a problem that we actually resolve any issue we're dealing with.

My quest kept taking me back, time and again, to the same answer for both the noisy mind in meditation, and the many life challenges clients shared with me in my role as a therapist.

What I saw was that our strong attachment to our program for getting love – our core program for life – had us creating a lot of images and expectations around what we wanted and how we wanted people, relationships, and the world to be. There were also a lot of desires and fears that came out of those images and expectations. All of this was, of course, fuel for the fire of a very busy, and often distracted, mind.

While the issues that the clients presented with were certainly real and needed to be addressed, the question was: Did the client want to just be free of the troubling symptoms, or were they willing to look deeper and actually resolve the real cause of what was going on in their life? Fortunately, with the personal growth movement coming into its own at that time, my clients were very much on board for looking deeper. You get to ask yourself the same question here: Do I want a quick fix or a permanent upgrade? Do I just want more space in my schedule, or do I want the exquisite ability to quiet my mind, alter time, and expand my ability to create at will?

Having done a great deal of work on myself, I was able to comfortably take my clients on that inner journey into their own "cave" where they learned to breathe into, acknowledge, express, and release any emotional backlog we ran into. Even though most of us have gotten pretty banged up at different times in our life, we consistently saw that the family of origin stuff was also the origin of the issues in their life, and that it was even the actual source of the current challenge they were dealing with.

I'd have to admit that more than a few of the people that I worked with had done some amazing work on themselves and they were also quite successful in many areas of their lives. As I listened to their stories of all the deep work they had already done, I more than a few times wondered what they expected me to be able to do. But, of course, that was my learning opportunity.

While the lives of these clients who had really done a great deal of work were going well, they each had a specific area that kept troubling them. To them it was like having three tires filled with air and the fourth sort of thumping along.

We breathed into their cave and took a look around at what, if any, unacknowledged emotional parts of themselves were still stuck and hiding in there. They looked at significant issues in their life, and would go through each looking to see if they had fully acknowledged, expressed, and released the anger, hurt, fear, guilt, or shame around each so that they could get to a place of understanding, appreciating, full forgiveness, and love.

It never took too long before we'd find the disparate part of themselves that had been left behind. In each and every case, they had done a great job of releasing almost all of the emotions connected to an issue with the exception of one. Sometimes it was shame and sometimes it was anger or fear, but every time I'd guide one of these unique individuals into their past, we'd find that piece that was still hanging them up. As they handled acknowledging, expressing, and releasing those lingering emotions, the anchor line was finally cut and they could set sail.

Discovering and recovering yourself:

If you do not heal your emotional backlog and rewrite your program for getting love to one of looking within for self-acceptance and approval, then your conscious mind (the 5% of your thoughts) can be in the present, but your subconscious mind (the 95% of your thoughts) will still be lost in the past or anticipating the future from a less than empowered place. In other words, your past will be determining your present, so you're essentially living in your energetic past.

You can focus your conscious mind on something that you want or a change that you want to create. For instance, "I want to drop 20 pounds," or "I want to write my legacy, life-changing book." But don't be surprised when your tsunami of subconscious thoughts unravels or sabotages your best intentions. The obvious thoughts that you are aware of might look like this: "I don't have time." "My team has overscheduled me again." "I've got another cold and am not at my best to follow through with my plan." Yet the subconscious thoughts that are quietly undermining your best intentions may sound something like this: "I'm afraid." "Who do you think you are?" or, "I'm not enough, it's not enough, there's never enough," or "You can't have it all."

I see this happen with people time and again. They practice some temporary or superficial method in an attempt to change the aggravating symptoms or circumstances in their life. But the change doesn't last. This symptom-chasing approach is really a disservice because the person diligently trying the latest guaranteed fix often begins to think that there must be something wrong with them. They worry that perhaps they really can't make those changes in their life and concede to a life of "good enough" out of not being able to make those shifts. A good example of this is the determined dieter who painstakingly drops the weight but then keeps gaining it all back and then some. While perhaps less obvious to others, many of us are experiencing this same thing around our own challenges.

To truly change, we need to heal and integrate those parts of ourselves that have been left in the past. We need to reconnect with them and give them the supportive parenting that they didn't receive before. Imagine being a parent and discovering that your child is lost. Now years later, on a dark and rainy night, you hear a hesitant knock on your front door. As you cautiously open it, you see your long-lost child standing there. You immediately see the tremendous pain and suffering they have endured. Do you slam the door and tell them to go away?

That's exactly what many people do when a part of their past comes back knocking. So many clients through the years tell me how they just want the problem to be over with. They just want it gone so that they never have to deal with it again. No matter how many times a disowned aspect of themself has knocked on the door, hoping for help, for understanding, for a warm, welcoming embrace, they'd shove that raw and painful part down – essentially slamming the door on their most vulnerable self – over and over again.

Perhaps your response to that wounded child on your doorstep scenario was that you would invitingly open the door and be thrilled to have had that child return. Can you fully embrace them and be willing to help them deal with and heal all that they have gone through? Will you be there with them and support them in acknowledging, fully expressing, and releasing their anger at you and at life? Can you be present with the depth of the hurt they feel at being abandoned and not cared for? Would you help them through the shame at what they have gone through and their feeling that maybe it was their fault that they'd been shut out? Maybe they feel like there must have been, or still is, something wrong with them, that caused you to let them become separated from you and lost?

Maybe you're asking if that inner child is really real. Over the years, as I have witnessed hundreds of clients doing a mirror exercise where they are talking to their inner child, I can only tell you that yes, our inner child is absolutely real. I can always tell when a client has made the connection, because the eyes reflected in the mirror appear to be a much younger version of the client's eyes. Anyone who has done this work will verify how real that inner child is to them.

With each part of yourself that you remember and reintegrate into the whole of who and what you are, you are accepting and loving all that you are. With that acceptance, you are becoming whole and able to more fully express your authentic self. I remember the first time I was faced with a lost part of myself. I reflexively wanted to shove away what felt like some entity trying to enter me. Through the years, though, as my healing continued, the discovery and opportunity to regain a disowned part of myself became more like a celebration.

Looking deeper –the five questions:

I imagine that you have done some deep work, so here is an exercise that you might find enjoyable, insightful, and rewarding. Be open with whatever and whomever comes forward. Some of your most deeply hidden, disowned parts of yourself may, at first, seem obscure and unrelated to your current situation or roles in your life. But like greeting the little lost child returning home on the rainy, dark night, be patient and welcoming. Turn on the porch light, be open to visitors, and just see who shows up. As you continue to accept, love, and integrate any disowned parts of yourself, you'll be amazed, as I was, at the sense of calm, completeness, and creativity that emerges. In addition to helping you love and accept all of who you are, integrating your disowned or "unacceptable" identities ultimately helps you quiet your mind and enhance and accelerate your ability to create.

Rather than having to wait for any parts of myself to feel safe enough to come forward, I decided to start my day with an exercise of inviting them to help me in my process of remembering and becoming whole. I'd just sit at my computer before my first client came and inwardly invite one part of my past, whoever felt ready, to come forward.

At first, the more familiar ones came up. One day it would be the dad in me, another the husband, then the Marine, and so on. As the weeks went on, the players became more obscure, like the one who felt ashamed about being emotional, or the one that could be a bit of a troublemaker. The even later ones turned out to be more challenged, like the very young one who had been sexually molested by a neighbor girl who was regularly babysitting me, or the one that felt my dad didn't like him. Many of the later ones I hadn't even known about, so it was a profound experience to get to meet them and invite them back into my life.

The five questions I'd ask each of them were:

1. Who are you?

2. How did you become separated?

   a. What were the circumstances or the event that went on?

3. What do you need and how can I help you to heal?

4. Do you want to rejoin and be a part of the whole again?

5. Who would you like us to be?

    a. This was a question about literally shifting my personality and sense of who I was and how I was leading my life. I recognized that the person typing was just a representative of who I was, and not necessarily who I'd become.

When you do the exercise, I'd recommend you just stay open to whomever comes forward and be willing to hear whatever they need to share. When it came to the question about what did they need so that they could heal, I found that I had an inner vision that changed or morphed with each newly-integrated self. What started off as an inner counseling office became a healing center on a pond in a nice size meadow surrounded by a forest. Those more frightened parts within me that felt rejected or really unwanted would come to the edge of the forest and, still hidden, would watch how things were going until they felt really safe. In time, when the collective would see someone coming in, they'd get everything prepared and make it as safe and inviting as possible. They wanted to make sure that those more vulnerable parts could see that they were not only very welcome but were valued pieces of the puzzle. They knew that with each returning part, we had an ever-clearer picture of who and what we were.

Of course, I know that this sounds crazy. It sounds like I'm acknowledging that I have multiple personalities, and I am, and I do. But perhaps, if you find the courage to accept and love yourself, you will find that you do, too. With time, the community merged into the oneness they had chosen to create, but I imagine the healing center is still there within me, just in case we have some late arrivals.

In summary:

The strength of our foundation, determined by the depth of the healing we have done, largely dictates the extent that we can fully explore our potential. While it happens in all fields, I have personally watched spiritual and personal growth leaders rise to national renown, only to have their unhealed issues catch up with them and destroy their lives. Unfortunately, in their rise and fall, they not only destroyed their own life but the lives of others who had trusted them.

Ignoring the opportunity to heal ourselves always catches up with us in one way or another. It may not be on the national stage, but it will play out in our relationships, our health, how happy and fulfilled we feel, or in some other significant way in our life.

Early on, I saw the power of doing the emotional work, but because all my spiritual and meditation teachers had sort of downplayed the impact of emotions and our past, I decided to dig a little deeper. I sought out and discussed this with the leaders of the Vedanta Center in Santa Barbara, with a Zen Master, and with several other monks and spiritual leaders. I shared with them what I was doing and the results I was getting. I wanted to know whether they felt the emotional work was really necessary, or if meditation alone could serve as that cleansing, enhancing, personal evolutionary process. Even though it was somewhat contrary to what they were teaching, every one of them confirmed that, "No, meditation alone is not enough, at least for those of us who have grown up and live in the west." and that I was on the right track.

It was decades later in reading Thich Nhat Hanh's interpretations of Buddha's talks (the Sutras) on breathing and mindfulness that I fully understood how meditation can and is meant to be used in healing the past. The healing work that I'd learned and developed was really just a much more accelerated way to do the work, and I appreciate both.

Just as we can't build a house on an unstable foundation, we can't expect to build a happy, fulfilling, and successful life with just the parts of us that were deemed acceptable by others. You know and share this in many ways. So, I appreciate you taking the opportunity to support both of us in remembering as we continue to heal and enjoy our amazing journey.

Chapter 5

Step 2: The Power of the Breath

"Feelings come and go like clouds in a windy sky.
Conscious breathing is my anchor."
–Thich Nhat Hanh

How fully we breathe determines how fully we live. To the extent that we inhale, we are welcoming in life. To the extent that we exhale, we are letting go and becoming more fully ourselves. The breath is essentially our innate "volume dial" that determines our level of consciousness, which completely colors how we view and experience life.

I was introduced many years ago to the power of breathing by Tom, who was using breathing in his work as a re-birther. Over time he continued to introduce me to even more esoteric breathing techniques, which resulted in my altering my focus from being a college English instructor to one of becoming a transformational therapist. All of this breath work had such a supportive and profound effect on me that I was hooked from the beginning.

It might sound strange, but the breath has become my greatest teacher and most trusted companion. It has taken me into and through some of the darkest corners of my past and into the most incredible levels of consciousness one can explore. While initially I was learning to breathe, over time I also learned to be breathed and become the breath. I can tell you from direct experience, there are some pretty magical realms available to you my friend.

It is common for me to hear from clients, even decades after our work together, how excited they still are about the empowering use of the breath. It's great to hear how over the top they are, as they share how much the breath has become a core part of their path. Being aware of how they were breathing helped them to be aware and take better care of themselves. They also found by using the breath to stay present, they were better able to be present with others and truly listen to what people were saying and understand what they were needing. While this enhanced all of their relationships, they particularly appreciated how it created a deeper, more connected and compassionate relationship with their significant partner and children. They also often share how, with their clearer focus and greater efficiency, they no longer feel like they're always late, hurried, or out of time.

As we were growing up and creating our program for getting love, we learned from our parents and others what feelings were okay to express and which ones needed to be denied and suppressed. Back in the day, boys were often taught that being afraid or crying were not the manly things to do, whereas girls were often shamed into stuffing down their anger. Shaming names were associated with and used for each. But almost all of us learned that, to get the acceptance and love we wanted, it was better to shove down and try to ignore at least some of who we naturally were and how we would otherwise normally express ourselves. We also often felt it was best to try to shove down at least one, if not several, of our emotions. So, as an example, any time I expressed any anger, fear, hurt, or shame, it resulted in creating more of a separation between my parents and myself. Since I wanted and needed that acceptance and love, I did my very best to not feel, display, or even acknowledge that I had those feelings. Don't get me wrong, I had great parents. I honestly couldn't have wished for better, but in their lives growing up, there just wasn't any room for acknowledging and expressing those emotions.

When young kids on the playground don't get what they want, it's not uncommon to see them go through a whole range of emotions, starting perhaps with anger about not immediately getting what they want, then fear that they might not get what they want, and hurt that they can't have it. In more volatile family situations, they can even go into feelings of guilt or shame that they've done something wrong or that, for some reason, they aren't worthy of having what they want or need.

Of course, if we are angry about something, but are not allowed to show it, we then get even angrier and more deeply hurt or fearful. We can even be unconsciously angry that we can't get angry, so a cycle of denial only builds up the backlog. All of these emotions over the years can get stuffed down and, over time, shut off from who we become. I know I thought I had a *Leave it to Beaver* childhood, so you can imagine my surprise when in workshop, a very deep-seated anger exploded out of me. I'd never seen my parents get angry with each other, so it was a totally alien emotion to me. Of course, over the years, my inner work has revealed layers of other emotions that I had suppressed as well.

From my early work as a client with Tom, and my own work through the years with thousands of clients, it became clear that one of the most effective and common ways for us to keep our emotions in check is to not breathe. It's amazing to watch how few short and shallow breaths a person typically takes, especially when they're in an uncomfortable situation. In a movie with Robert De Niro called *The Mission*, he is a soldier who is doing his best to become a priest. Part of this transitional journey for him involves him carrying all of his old body armor and weaponry with him as he scales steep cliffs and treks through the jungle in search of souls to save. At one point, as he is reaching the top of a very difficult climb, his armor drops off and he has to go all the way back down to retrieve it and scale the cliff again. It was such a classic metaphor for how we hang onto our emotional backlog and all of our past that we were unable to emotionally process. It's as if we are literally stuck to that past that we didn't know how to move beyond. So much of our energy goes toward hanging on to and inwardly struggling with the past, which exhausts us of our energy. This often happens on a subconscious level, such that we don't even know we're doing it. We're not as focused or able to be present and deal with what is presently going on in our life. It often shows up as not taking as good of care of ourselves as we'd like or in our not having enough time or energy to get things done that are actually very important to us. It's like running the Boston Marathon with one leg tied behind your back. It's hard to keep up.

On my own path and as a therapist I, of course, use the breath to open up and be able to go within. There are different breathing techniques that facilitate helping us get in touch with our past and acknowledge, express, and release the emotional backlog that is held there. By freeing up that emotional backlog, we can use the energy – that we'd been using to keep those unacceptable emotions stuffed down – to now open ourselves up and move forward in our life.

Being a sailor, a metaphor I relate to is one of seeing ourselves as a beautifully built sailboat capable of enjoying wondrous adventures. The only problem is that we are attached to an anchor (a past event or issues) that is lodged in the depths that we can't even see. The anchor line (the unhealed emotions we have tied to that event or issue) keeps us bound and sailing in limiting circles. Most people try to reconcile this limitation by convincing themselves that sailing within this circle is all they really want. Whatever emotions, interactions, and experiences lie within the range of this circle becomes their known – their comfort zone.

Some of us, though, feel like there is so much more that we want to see, do, and be, that we begin to recognize this anchor as a limitation. The anchor is often a collection of past events that keeps us playing small. For some, it is a major event that they can identify, such as events around having an alcoholic parent, a personal trauma, or having lost someone they loved. You may have heard many of your contemporary leaders say, "The past is the past. You can't change it, so don't waste any time or energy focusing on it." But they're missing the whole point and short-changing anyone who is being called to "more" in and from their life. Yes, you can't change what happened in the past, but you can go in and embrace (rather than resist) those defining events, so that you can see, feel, and heal those buried emotions that will otherwise keep you tethered.

While some try to pull up the anchor and erase the past through various quick fix techniques, it is much more effective to simply acknowledge, express, and release the emotions, which are like the anchor line that keeps that lovely sailboat (you) tethered to that limiting anchor. When we acknowledge and heal our inner child and past emotions, we are freeing ourselves to live boldly and sail into our dreams. You literally free up more energy, focus, and heightened mental ability to do the things that are most important to you in your life. Last week, a client who is just a little over halfway through the first step of this overall process, excitedly shared with me, "…and I thought I was smart before!" As a successful attorney, she is very bright, but as she clears up her backlog, it's like someone lifting up the dimmer switch. She's realizing the "more" of who she has always been. It's so cool to witness people discovering themselves.

The breath is quite literally the most powerful and effective tool to use for this process. The breath is like the catalyst for the other aspects of the work. The past then truly does become just the past and not something that is determining our future.

While not breathing fully is a great tool to keep our emotions in check, it has some serious downsides. The obvious one is that we are not inhaling nearly as much energizing and blood-purifying oxygen as we need to optimize how our body and brain are functioning. Not fully breathing in and cleansing our blood, of course, results in a decrease in immune function and susceptibility to disease. We don't have as much energy as we'd otherwise have, we get more colds, headaches, and body pains, and we can even age faster over time.

A perhaps more serious result of our not breathing fully is that the stress we are putting on our body communicates with our brain that we are stressed. This signal turns off our rest and digest parasympathetic nervous system and turns on our fight, flight, or freeze sympathetic nervous system. In times of real trouble, we definitely want our sympathetic nervous system to kick in and prepare us for surviving a threatening situation, but, if it is staying on most of the time, then all the organ functions that the parasympathetic system handles are thrown off.

So, when we're not fully and comfortably breathing, and our sympathetic system takes over, we can experience poor digestion, irritability, and poor-quality sleep, and even stubborn weight gain in the belly, just to name a few. Keep in mind that the brain is also wanting to kick into fight or flight, which means we're going to have trouble being present and consciously creating our life. In other words, restricting your breathing so that you can keep your emotional backlog stuffed down, can significantly disrupt and decrease your quality of life. Your body, highest goals, happiness, and vitality all suffer when you're not breathing supportively. Look at the primary health problems of old age, and you'll have a good list of how our quality and quantity of life are altered.

So, if you feel like you don't have enough time to take care of yourself, nurture your significant relationship, or get that book or special project done, you might want to go in and find out if you're emotionally clear. You'd also want to do this inner work so that you can breathe more fully, which gives you more awareness, energy, and time to enjoyably conduct your happy, successful life. There are also many other benefits, but for now we'll stick with what's relevant to your immediate challenge.

As Einstein shared with us, "Time is relative." I had studied the martial arts before and while I was in the Marines, and I felt pretty confident that I could handle myself. So, when I was standing in front of my maybe 110-pound tai chi teacher, and he asked me to attack him, I was hesitant, to say the least. Finally, he assured me he would be alright, and so in I went. All I can remember is that at first it was like he was a ghost. He was always right in front of me, but I couldn't even touch him.

While I was moving at full speed, he was moving in slow motion. After the whole class quit laughing, he shared with us his secret of how being very present and conscious allowed him to literally slow time – to see and to sense every move before it was even made. People talk about how time slows down in something like a car accident or how time flies by when you're having fun. I can also tell you for sure, that the older I get, the faster time seems to pass.

So, if time is relative, then maybe, just maybe, it's not that you don't have enough time, but that something else may be going on with you. So, let's do a quick inventory here. What emotions might you be keeping down and still in check? How fully and deeply do you breathe on a regular basis, even when you're not thinking about it? How is your digestion, your mood, your sleep, and your overall health?

I know that you have done a lot of work on yourself to get where you are, but, like everyone else, the opportunities to heal a little more just keep on coming. As you well know, the more we resist or ignore growth opportunities, the more dramatic they become the next time around. If you find that you don't have enough time to take good care of yourself, then that's at least one indicator that it's a good time to look a little deeper within.

If you are willing, take a moment and let yourself draw in a nice deep breath. Now, let yourself sit up comfortably straight with your shoulders relaxed, and notice how, as you expand your belly out, you draw in a nice full breath. As you draw the breath in, let yourself notice how good it feels. Let yourself continue to focus on each breath you are taking. Allow your shoulders to drop. Feel how your belly expands out with each inhale and naturally deflates with each exhale.

As you continue to breathe, you may want to explore extending your exhale a little more during and with the next three breaths. Nice, now just let yourself stay with it for another minute or two. You might notice that it's like when someone gently rubs your shoulders for a moment and you hope they'll stay with it at least a little, if not a lot, longer. It can kind of be like getting a taste of your favorite ice cream and realizing how good a bowl of it would be. Breathing is really good!

You might begin to appreciate that you have quieted down for a moment and become more present. Your mind is perhaps a bit more relaxed and maybe even quieter. Maybe you're noticing how you're feeling, or perhaps thinking about how you'd like to do this a bit more often - if you just had the time....

The STOP process:

That's the great thing about breathing: We become more focused and present. There is a process we used back in the early 80s at the Brain Integration Center that we called the "STOP" process. You may have heard of it. It's a simple little technique you can use whenever you're feeling uncomfortable or challenged by something.

The first step is to **stop** for a moment.

The second step is to then **take** several gentle deep breaths.

The third step is to **observe** what's going on and what you're feeling. Notice what your best next available step is.

And, as you continue to breathe, the fourth step is to **proceed** forward, taking that best next step.

So, **STOP** = **s**top, **t**ake several deep breaths, **o**bserve, and then **p**roceed. It's as easy as that. What people notice is, that when they slow down or stop for a moment and take in a few breaths, they become more present and aware. In that present state of heightened awareness, they can take a look around and see more clearly what is actually going on in their life and what they are feeling and needing at that time. With this information, they can see what their best options are and what their best next step is. They can then trust and proceed, taking appropriate action in their life.

While in the beginning this sounds like a time out, but with practice it all can happen in the blink of a breath and become a very helpful "time in." If you actually keep on breathing and let yourself stay in that more conscious and aware place, you will greatly enhance your life. You will be living in the present. It can become a lifestyle that supports you in having the time to take care of yourself, appreciate and nurture your significant relationship, and do an amazing job getting that special project done that takes you and your work up to the next level.

One reason you may not be getting that coveted project done is because, if it is a real game-changer, you may only be capable of creating it if and when you shift to a higher level. Simply put, the "you" that you are now, in this current place, may not be able to do what's required. Perhaps more time isn't really what you need. Perhaps you are just resisting evolving with the changes that your life is offering you. If you breathe and go in and find out what gifts await you, you may find that what you discover is the perfect gift to shift you up to your next level in life. From that expanded, energetic awareness and place of being, taking care of yourself or getting that special project done becomes a fun thing that you enjoy doing.

Using the breath as an elevator:

I often fondly remember a Swiss student of mine, who not only learned but went on to teach the material I'd shared. At the young age of 35, he was diagnosed with cancer. Even with the tremendous care from the hospital and the support from his wonderful wife, family, and friends, he realized he would be dying soon. For a couple of weeks, the extra bed in his room became my home. It was so inspiring to witness how he used all that he had learned so that he could be absolutely present in the final days of his life. The joy and love that we all felt and that filled that room, came to a climax at the time of his death as he sat chanting, meditating, and literally radiating joy and light. I watched as he used his breath to rise above the fear and pain, letting go of life to rise up to a level of mastery I have seldom witnessed. I watched as he breathed through the darkness and literally into the light. At his death, everyone was filled with love and overwhelmed into a state of laughing, crying, and celebrating Christian's life. He became my teacher, and showed me how to take this path into a full, loving life, spectacular finale, and expanded "next" that is available to all of us.

So, a way to appreciate the value of the breath is to see it almost like an elevator that can take you to whatever level you want to go to. The great thing about having this amazing vehicle is that there is no need to get attached to any particular level. This allows you to feel at home throughout existence and beyond. And the most wonderful thing of all, is that your breath is always right there with you to use as you wish.

Keep in mind that the more of the deeper work that you have done, the easier and more enjoyable your evolution becomes. Going deeply within is often the scariest thing for many people to imagine doing, but the worst-case scenario is and always will be that they come out with greater levels of acceptance and love for themselves. This enhanced inner connection always becomes mirrored in their relationships with others and within their work in the world.

Doing the inner work, for me, had once seemed like a terrifying experience, but it has since become one of the most magical and empowering experiences I know. Over the years, like many, I have learned that the more challenging the experience, the greater the reward.

Just as the breath is a major player in step one, seeing the source of any challenge and resolving deeper issues (as I hope you came to recognize in chapter four), you will see how important it is in the other steps as well.

In the next chapter, we'll be looking at how to neurologically upgrade, access, and be able to integrate whole brain thinking. To do this successfully, we need to have at least resolved our core programming. This means we have sufficiently healed and rewritten our program for getting love, so that we are now looking for greater acceptance and love within our self, rather than outside from others. We also will need to know how to use the breath to bring us into a quieter, more mindful state.

The Centering Breath:

While there are many useful breathing techniques for a variety of results, we'll be primarily going over what is most supportive for evolving into and through transitions to a more empowered and loving place. I do recognize that you may be an advanced meditator and/or may already know how to use the breath in some unique ways. I am not saying those aren't effective; I'm just suggesting you be open to expanding your tool box and exploring additional ways to use the tools that you already have.

To help with developing your focus and quieting the mind, I'd suggest you start by sitting up comfortably straight and taking a few deep, gentle breaths.

Sitting up comfortably straight opens up your airway, allows you to more fully fill your lungs, and helps you to stay aware and focused. When we take in a full deep breath, the belly will expand out like a balloon, and your shoulders will stay open and relaxed.

As you let yourself relax and breathe, just enjoy watching how perfectly your body is designed for this. As you draw in the breath through your nose, feel how your belly expands out, and then, after a moment, your belly naturally relaxes as the breath is released. In, through and out, again and again.

As you draw breath in, it fills the lungs and is taken by the blood throughout the body. As those cells distribute the energy of the breath, they also pick up the waste or CO_2 you'll release during your exhale. It's so simple that it's easy to miss how truly amazing this entire process is.

The plants and trees take in the CO_2 that we exhale and they, in turn, release the oxygen that we need to breathe in. That breath is a part of everything and it is part of how you are connected with everything. It is your life force and so much more. As you continue to gently breathe in and out through your nose, feel the natural rhythm that unfolds.

And as you breathe, continue to inhale through your nose, and begin to now exhale through your open mouth. In through your nose, filling your lungs, and then out through your open mouth, again and again. There is no need to effort or force, just let yourself naturally breathe in and out, enjoying the flow of energy.

Staying with the breathing and inhaling through your nose, begin to extend your exhale out of your mouth. In through the nose and slowly exhaling out through your open mouth, focusing on the flow of energy, moving in, through, and out, again and again.

As you continue to breathe and extend your exhale, begin to ever so slightly constrict your throat area during and with each exhale. As you make that area somewhat restricted, you will hear a shift in the sound of the breath as it moves through your throat area and then out. Just stay with this for a few more breaths.

Good, and now as you begin to relax and return to your normal breathing pattern, perhaps close your eyes and feel how you feel. How is your mind doing – how does your body feel? Just notice and breathe. Just breathe and relax.

Good job! When you are feeling anxious, stressed, or just wanting to quiet your mind so that you can focus and concentrate, this breath is a great tool. You can do it a few times or for a more extended period of time. It will generally relieve headaches and allow you to relax, will help with falling asleep, and even when something is getting you riled up. You may find that you don't need medications or drugs, or even a time out, as you begin to use this style of breathing to get calm, focused, and present, and to use your time a great deal more effectively.

Proactive self-clearing:

If you are more proactive, as I tend to be, then you might want to play with a little something that I do from time to time, which is to just sit and breathe. You can do this for an hour or whatever amount of time you're willing to invest in yourself. I have my daily meditation practice, but, when I do this particular deep review and clearing out process, I generally sit for about five to six hours. To support my experience, I'll go to one of my favorite places in nature or just get comfy in my meditation room. The idea is to plan on literally keeping your butt on the pillow for the entire time.

While in my daily meditation I am generally focused on journeying into the silence and then letting go, this practice is, at least in the earlier part, somewhat like taking an inventory of what's going on in my life and in the world. I like to sit up straight and have my eyes closed, with my focus being primarily on going within and slowing my thoughts.

A way to think about sitting like this is that the noisier your mind is, the noisier your focus will need to be. A friend of mine has a Hindu ashram in the

Swiss Alps, and I'll never forget the first time I sat with them. They start off by loudly banging on pots and pans, creating an absolute racket. At some point, they'd all stop and immediately go into meditation. I have to admit, while at first it seemed crazy, it absolutely worked. So, whatever approach works for you is fine. You may, perhaps, want to have some meditative music playing in the background.

I usually start off by chanting "Om" for an extended time, to help me get both centered and clear. I will at some point automatically shift to chanting "sring" and again continue that for a while. These are both favorites left over from my Hindu days. If you have a favorite chant or sound, I'm sure they will serve you in much the same way. It's all about the vibration and extended focus.

After I have chanted for a time (the noisier my mind is, the longer I'll chant) and am feeling quieter and more vibrationally clear, I'll move into breathing. As I am chanting and breathing, I just let my mind be open and explore how I'm feeling and how I'm doing on ever-deeper levels. As different aspects of my life – say relationships, my service, plans, or politics – come forward, I just stay present and, from a place of curiosity, watch.

The first breath I'd generally use is the inhaling through the nose and extending the exhale through the open mouth style that we just explored above. Again, as you do this, just slightly constrict the throat. You will hear the difference as the breath moves through the still relaxed, yet slightly more constricted area. Start with focusing on the breath as it moves through the throat area, later as it moves out of your mouth, and then, still later, as it is expressed into the Universe.

As I breathe more and more deeply into an area of life or into my cave, I can, from time to time, feel my breathing getting caught on something, so I'll focus on and breathe into whatever it is until it feels clear again. If the snag is substantial enough, I might even go back into the chanting to get through it. Sometimes I'll become aware of or see images of what is going on, and other times it's more just a feeling.

As you explore your conscious and subconscious mind you can also shift to slowing your breathing as you inhale in through your nose, and then slowly, extending your exhale, into your closed mouth. This, along with shifting your core programming (from chapter four) is also part of neurologically rewiring and integrating your brain that leads to whole brain thinking, which we will go over in the following chapter. I'd also recommend you still keep your throat area slightly constricted during this style of breathing. Touch the tip of your tongue very gently to the back of your upper teeth and slowly extend the time of each exhale. You may want to play with the length that you extend each exhale, which also deepens your focus and experience. This is also known as the ujjayi breath (victory breath) which translates "to be victorious."

You might want to use the open mouth exhale more for breathing into and through interruptions and distractions. This type of breathing quickly releases and moves the energy. It is useful as a detox and releasing tool. The closed mouth exhale is quite useful for expanding your awareness of yourself and existence. As your mind becomes quieter and moves beyond focusing on the this's and that's of your life, you'll notice that exhaling into the closed mouth serves you well. As you get even more still and quiet, you can just move into a natural soft belly breathing.

When you start this overall process, you are most likely in your everyday Beta brainwave or waking state. You're aware of what's going on around you and taking that information in and figuring out what to do with it. But, as you continue with your chanting and breathing, your brain waves will slow down into a more relaxed Alpha state brainwave pattern. These waves are a bit longer and not as frequent.

As you move from the chanting into the more extended breathing, you will slow your brain waves down even further, as you enter the Theta state. In the quiet of the slower Theta brainwaves you can begin to access and, with experience, reprogram your previously subconscious thoughts. This is how approaches like hypnosis are able to work.

As you continue to breathe and let go, breathe and go more deeply within, you will be entering a Delta brain wave state where you have even greater access, understanding, and the ability to rewire your subconscious thoughts. As your subconscious thoughts are revealed and you become more aware of them, you can begin to let go of any old, unsupportive patterns and begin upgrading your system. After you do the deeper work, and can more easily quiet your mind, this process is a great maintenance care routine.

I know of a few techniques that the most advanced Tibetan monks use in deep meditation over years of practice to heal deeper issues. From their point of view, these issues may be from your karmic past or from this current lifetime. The caveat is something like what the great Tibetan monk, Dudjom Lingpa, shared, "Only those who have stored vast collections of merit, in many ways, over incalculable eons, will encounter this path." (from B. Alan Wallace's book, *Stilling the Mind)*. In other words, yes, this meditation process could work for you, but it could take you a few eons.

If you want to cut those eons down to a more workable time frame, then take a look at these five steps that I have been fortunate enough to have learned through decades on the path, and you'll be on your way. If you're looking for a quick fix meditation process, there are plenty of good apps for your phone that can help you with that. Sorry for getting a little side-tracked, but the quick fixes are a sensitive area for me. I only want to share what I know will work for you over a lifetime, not just for a short while.

If you're looking at healing the deeper causes and having lasting change, then perhaps it's time for your Hero's Journey. Like the repeat dieter who keeps gaining back the weight, it's hard to watch those who don't get to the source of their healing come to a place where they feel like there is something wrong with them because they feel like they keep falling short and bumping up against the same old stuff.

As you have seen, I'll be introducing you to a variety of breathing styles, and each one draws you into a particular level of consciousness. So, as you breathe more deeply, and later more expansively, you will find yourself shifting into different breathing styles as you move into and through the various levels. Of course, "deeply" and "expansively" really become the same thing, but this is just a way to talk about it.

This kind of inner clearing helps you to notice and release any potential issues or challenges that may be developing. In proactively acknowledging and breathing into what is stirring within your energy field, you greatly diminish future drama. As you move deeper into the silence, you will also find windows and doorways that give you insight and openings for taking your life up to the next level. Ultimately, it's nice to just bathe into the silence and let go, beyond any awareness of self. No worries about losing your way – you'll generally find yourself drifting back in at some point.

Your inner game:

One of the wonderful things about being a human being is that we get to choose the level of awareness and consciousness from which we want to live. If a person enjoys drama and stress, then we all know that it takes very little effort to have that. But if you are looking for a more centered, mindful life, then doing the work and learning to supportively breathe will lead you in that direction.

When I was Executive VP of Tim Gallwey's Inner Game Corporation, Tim was using his mindfulness techniques while working on the tennis court with Alan, a powerful L.A. attorney. Alan had a strong tennis game, but a very weak serve. To help him, Tim set several tennis ball cans at various points around one side of the court and had Alan try to hit them with overhead serves.

The attorney breathed into a focused place and did an impeccable job of smashing a can with each killer serve. The lesson was: Breathe and focus – get out of your head and you'll have a killer serve. And he did. A couple of days later, Alan showed up for his coaching and Tim asked him to hit a few serves. Expecting to see the powerhouse serves he'd seen the last time, Tim was stunned to see that he was back to using his old wimpy serve.

When Tim asked him why he wasn't using his new serve, Alan explained how he didn't understand how he had been able to serve like that and felt more comfortable with his old, lobbing serve.

Perhaps you're becoming aware that your established serve isn't powerful enough to be able to do what you truly want to be doing. It may be time for you to let go one more time and trust your higher self to serve up your life. With each evolution in your life you have a choice. Do you struggle and try to live from where you have grown comfortable, or do you breathe, and in a state of presence, see your best next step and take it?

We'll get into even greater benefits from the breath as we move into the remaining chapters. But for now, consider that your lack of time may be a supportive indicator that a very real growth opportunity is just waiting for you. It may be time for you to again peel another layer of the onion and breathe into a more supportive way of being – into a more focused, quiet, and aware inner place where you can enjoy and discover the extra time that you hadn't even noticed before.

I know. I have gone through this myself more times that I can remember. But for now, I'm just here to help you remember what you most likely already know. I'm just sharing with you what I know absolutely works. This 5 Steps of Personal Evolution process will not only resolve your challenges of not having enough time, but will become an invaluable asset for the rest of your marvelous journey. Breathe on!

Chapter 6

Step 3: Evolutionary Thinking

"It's not what you look at that matters, it's what you see."
—Henry David Thoreau

As a young adult while getting my Master's degree in English, I was invited to work in a learning center and teach at Compton Community College in East Los Angeles. It turned out to be one of those perfect opportunities in life. I had been a terrible student until I got out of the Marine Corps and I'm not just being humble when I share with you that my first two texts that I bought for myself were a math book that started with 1+1 and a primary grammar English book. It turns out that spending years in public school looking out of the window all day and never opening a book didn't really get me the education I needed.

At 21 years old, I was married to my high school sweetheart, and we had a bouncing baby boy. The American dream, right? Working at the boatyard for five dollars an hour was not going to cut it, so somewhere deep inside I decided that I had to get my ass in gear and make up for the twelve years that I'd skated through school. I was confident enough in my abilities that I knew that, if I applied myself, I would do well in my course work. At that time in my life, getting a degree seemed important, so I could better take care of my family. So, I started taking night classes at the local college after work. Within a couple years, I had gotten an A in calculus and a few years after that, I was working toward my Master's degree in English.

What happened in a compressed amount of time was that I learned how to learn. What I didn't realize in that process was that I was also learning to teach others how to learn. It wasn't until I actually arrived at Compton to teach English that I realized what a rough neighborhood and depressed economy it was – not exactly the ideal teaching or learning environment! Yet I completely appreciated where my learning-challenged students were coming from and believed I could help them grasp the value of education. Just as I had figured out how to learn, I could help them understand and use what they were learning to create their dreams.

This was a few years after the L.A. Watts riots, and Compton is right next to Watts, so those kids had more than a few hurdles growing up. In my Creative Writing class, I had the students write papers on the challenges they had faced in their young lives. Let me tell you, it was tough reading. I had each of my students set a goal for what they wanted to accomplish through their writing, so the subject matter they chose was always relevant and important to them.

One particular moment still stands out for me. I remember coming into the class one day and noticing a Black Panther newspaper on my desk. There on the front page was a feature article written by Jamal – one of my creative writing students. This particular young man had more than a few challenges throughout his school years and had to work even harder than most to be able to express himself. But he had one particular dream that drove him – he had always wanted to write for the Black Panther paper. As I stood there reading his article, fully taking in this young man's accomplishment, Jamal walked into the room. I smiled proudly and gave him a thumbs-up. Tears welled up in both of our eyes, as he was being seen and heard in the way that he wanted, perhaps for the first time in his life. This deeply moving moment made all of both of our efforts so worthwhile.

After several years, when I moved on to teaching at another college, I took what I had learned from my students at Compton and became instrumental in creating and running another learning center. While the school was closer to my hometown of Newport Beach, there were a lot of young people at that school who had recently fled from Vietnam. They were what, at the time, were referred to as "the boat people," as that is how they'd escaped from their country. They were often dealing with the loss of family members and their homeland, along with having to learn a new language and trying to get accustomed to living in America.

My success in helping these immigrant ESL (English as a second language) kids, as well as the other students in my creative writing classes, had me seriously looking at the big question of, "How do we learn?" The journey began. While working on my PhD, I was introduced to an incredible woman named Carol Austin. She was teaching at an alternative university and running The Brain Integration Center in Encinitas, California. She was the real deal, a teacher extraordinaire. With the help of her daughter Hillary, Carol was helping people understand the primary functions of the brain's left and right hemispheres, and what we then referred to as the mammalian (mid-brain) and reptilian (brainstem) brains. Participants began to understand how they used their brain and how they could neurologically upgrade, access, and integrate their entire brain so that it was functioning as a more integrated whole.

Carol had already developed a successful Brain Integration drawing workshop, and, working as her co-director, we also developed programs together around writing and communication. The dyslexic, and other learning challenged kids we worked with went from struggling to land a D or C grade, to being awarded A's and B's. They were also more centered and calm, showing up with better attitudes and more confidence. In our clients who came to us with brain damage, we were witnessing them neurologically rewire the remaining parts of their brain and gradually regaining most of what they had thought they'd lost. What later became known as "neuroplasticity" was a concept that we took for granted and put to practice with our clients long before it was ever named and proven with current hard science.

I recall one of our clients chuckling at himself as he reflected back on what an overbearing presence he used to be. Manny was a big, burly, Samoan man, self-described as a very serious, intentionally intimidating, high-powered attorney. Manny came to us after having lost much of his left-brain function from severe head trauma he sustained in a near-fatal car crash. The left-brain harbors linear thinking. Its functioning is crucial for the systematic skills and thought patterns necessary for a high-powered trial attorney. Manny knew his career was over. He started out feeling hopeless and was filled with despair – afraid that he would never have a fulfilling and meaningful life again. With his whole future at stake, Manny consistently practiced the brain integration exercises and techniques that Carol and I had developed. Within several months, his right brain began to take over many of those seemingly lost, linear skills that his left-brain had previously handled. Manny was becoming quite functional again, although his overall nature had changed into someone much softer and gentler in his manner – more creative, and expressive.

While Manny was eventually able to successfully work and take care of himself after such a big life trauma, there were unexpected perks that came out of our work together that he'd never imagined. It turned out that living with a newly integrated, remapped brain had opened up a whole new world of deeper, more meaningful relationships and creative artistic expression through painting, both of which Manny found incredibly satisfying. Manny told us that, in an odd sort of way, he was grateful for his "terrible accident" and wouldn't change a thing because of the new man he'd become.

The success of the Brain Integration Center caught the attention of personal growth "gurus" in and throughout the personal growth field. It wasn't long before we were trading advanced trainings and co-creating workshops with Tom Gordon (Parent Effectiveness Training) and many other of the big players of the day. During our extended workshops in the Tahoe area, the top thought leaders of those early days in the personal growth movement were invited to come together and share their insights and tools for transformation. I had the privilege of presenting on stage with Buckminster Fuller and other trailblazers who were pushing the envelope of learning and personal growth.

Neuroscience was in its infancy compared to the work they are doing today, but the lucky thing is that all these yet-to-be proven concepts and content we were teaching back then, turned out to be right. The work we were doing was based on the research and findings of the National Institute of Mental Health. Even the head of this very conservative Institute acknowledged that by fully integrating the right and left hemispheres, one is able to access the area of the brain where "the stuff of angels" is made. Since we were getting such great results, we didn't question the validity of our work at the time, but it has still been quite satisfying to watch the scientific proof unfold behind it.

While I describe my transformative approach in steps here in this book, it's really more of an emergence of ever-higher functioning, where you progressively access more and more of your own greater potential. Healing your emotional backlog and rewriting your program for getting love always result in a quieter mind. And with a quieter mind, you are able to be more focused, and more efficiently and effectively get things done. You literally have more time because you waste less time. This is true even as you evolve into the subtlest levels of healing your past. As you learn to breathe into an even more centered and mindful place, you become more present and aware. As you bring that presence and awareness together in an integrated brain, you not only access whole brain thinking, but also greater imagination and creativity. As the mind quiets, you can begin to hear and trust your intuition. You begin to tap your true innate capabilities. This heightened place of awareness and functioning is where the new, innovative, quantum leaps come from. In this place, you are able to imagine and create a way to move into and grow with and from whatever is coming into your life. It's all a gift!

It's easier to understand how this all works when you view the whole evolutionary progression. It's as if the same person goes from experiencing life as an assembly line employee, just doing their repeated task, to gaining a bigger picture and being the line manager, who sees to the assembly of an idea or action from start to the finish. With a mindful, integrated-whole brain, you expand from being a manager to being the CEO who has the bigger picture of what's going on, both generally in your field and in your specific area. The CEO not only sees the big picture (right brain) but is able to consciously select the most rewarding path toward their chosen goal (left brain). Like a Peyton Manning on the football field, a more conscious CEO is able to access and take in everything that is going on and use it all to successfully play and ultimately win the game.

And with practice, you – like me and like any master in their field – will learn to access this multi-dimensional higher functioning in merely a breath or two. It becomes an intuitively spontaneous practice that allows you to shift almost instantly to any level you choose. Being present and mindful with yourself and your partner or letting the perfect next step for accomplishing your project come to you (rather than chasing around in your brain to find it), enhances your ability to more fully enjoy your relationships and your work. Time becomes a gift and your friend that's there to support you, rather than an elusive commodity and a source of daily stress. You will find yourself automatically breathing where others might freeze. You become curious and aware rather than contracting with fear. You become more mindful and focused where others would normally become distracted. Ultimately, you just trust and look for the gift in whatever comes. You don't respond from a place of scarcity; rather you know that you're in an abundant universe, so you trust that whatever comes to you is an opportunity to more fully integrate and express the highest and best of who and what you are.

Even though you are clearly playing on the CEO level, no matter where we have gotten to in life, there is always another level of letting go that we can and need to do so that we can take our life and work up to that next level. There are many quick fixes for challenges, like not having enough time, but, as you well know, those quick fixes are only temporary solutions for specific situations. So, the question we need to address is: How do we see what we can't see; how do we get back into the flow when the water feels choppy?

Let me remind you of a little secret: The choppy water is not really "out there." What keeps us bouncing around and out of the flow lies within. Healing your emotional backlog and rewriting your program for getting love leads to a quieter mind. As you acknowledge, express, and release your emotional backlog, you diminish or shut off the old emotional triggers. All of those neurons that for so long had fired together and wired together, now become like an abandoned road that goes unused. You don't need to have some technique to avoid the old subconscious patterns, as those old neuronal pathways are no longer being reinforced. And when those old pathways aren't firing together, they cease to remain wired together and will eventually be re-used for a different and better purpose. There's no need to try to repair the old road. You're off on a whole different, smoother road – purposefully and efficiently cruising your new super-highway.

This means that your brain is actually working better and functioning at a higher level. You're no longer consciously or unconsciously distracted by subconscious thoughts of the past or the future. You are breathing, present, and focused. You are more in the zone rather than being distracted by the "what if's" and the "hows" and so much more. That gives you the advantage of seeing the optimal pathway through the jungle of options. You're no longer following a map that is weathered and stained with the past and future distractions; you have your own GPS that's guiding you along your path.

Any lack of integration that we have within our brain is due to the neglect of parts of ourselves that got stuck earlier in our life, when they/we weren't able to emotionally deal with something that was going on in our life. They basically got left behind and that disconnection within ourselves was reflected in our disconnection within our brain. Of course, the parts that others found acceptable and loveable during our enculturation period thrived and became our dominant brain pattern. So, in truth, integrating and being able to fully use our whole brain, is just a continuation of the healing that we've done in Step 1.

You shift your focus from looking outside of yourself for love and answers, to looking where they can actually be found – within. You are then developing new neuronal pathways that look for evidence that you do love and accept yourself. You have new perspectives and are developing new neural pathways that lead to maintaining a quieter mind and a more present way of living.

I remember, years ago, the owner of a little bookstore in town asked me to choose a small card from a stack. It turned out to be an Angel Card. On the card that I'd chosen, there was a cute little picture of an elfish angel and the word "Gratitude." It wasn't until later that I began to consider the word and decided to take an inward look at what I was feeling grateful for in my life. I was standing at my favorite point in the harbor, and so the view of the islands and sunset was a good start, but the list seemed rather short. As I started doing a gratitude exercise each day, the depth of my feelings and the list of what I was grateful for grew. Within a couple of weeks, it was a sacred moment I enjoyed each day. Years later, I still often stand on that point and enjoy the depth of gratitude I have for every aspect of my life. The point is that within weeks, the brain had begun to neurologically rewire itself and look for supportive information. That same incredible plasticity of your brain will have you looking for and at all the reasons that you fully accept and love yourself. This is like taking your foot off the brake of your life and accelerating into your new life. Time becomes a tool you enjoy using, rather that something that you're at the effect of. You are enjoying a more mindful way of living.

Living your life from a place of mindful presence makes it easier to integrate and access your whole brain. As you continue this integrative process, there is little, if any, resistance to your developing the new neuronal freeways you'll need for the higher levels of imagination, creativity, and intuition. Keep in mind what Albert Einstein shared, "*Imagination* is more important than knowledge. For knowledge is limited, whereas *imagination* embraces the entire world, stimulating progress, giving birth to evolution."

The circuits between and within the different aspects of the brain will set up enhanced communication pathways that allow them to work as a synchronous, fully integrated, and optimized system. You have literally upgraded your brain and the abilities of your mind. We'll take a look at where you can go from there in the next couple of chapters.

The key point here is, that with this full cascade of higher functioning you'll enjoy, your whole system will, in effect, be upgraded. Within this higher level of perception, creative problem solving, and reception, you will use your time more effectively and manifest even greater results. You will be more productive, working smarter rather than harder, and find that you have more time to take care of yourself, to devote to your relationships, and to creatively invest in that special project.

I do get that it absolutely feels like your problem is that you're overscheduled by your own success. And while that is true on one level (at the choppy surface level), I consistently see that when we quell the agitation and resistance within, when we re-establish our inner current and flow, the choppy surface of our life just naturally settles down. Perhaps you're beginning to see that it's not so much a lack of time that's the biggest problem, but that you need to take yourself up to the next level in order to be able to manage it all and still develop that next project or write that next book. As we get out of our own way – and become clearer on who we want and need to be to play on that higher level we are being called to – we end up creating the space for it all.

A brain integrating process:

As a model for you to more fully understand and appreciate the process of integrating the two hemispheres of your brain, we'll take a look at an overview of the drawing workshop that much of my later brain integration work was modeled after.

Participants first are told to draw something like a pumpkin or a tree. Like school kids do, most of the drawings look like the classic images of each. This becomes sort of their "before" reference piece. From that point on, there are three main areas I train people in, that set the stage for the left and right hemispheres to be able to creatively collaborate: becoming present, learning to see, and learning to trust the brain's innate skills. Throughout the workshop, clients draw a variety of objects in various ways, using each hand and both hands together.

The right brain is generally thought of as being more creative, but the truth is that each of the hemispheres really has their own style. As I imagine you know, the left and right brain are connected by the corpus callosum, which is wonderfully designed as an information highway between the two halves of the cerebrum. The left hemisphere controls the right side of the body and the right hemisphere controls the left side. This is why you can use the movement of each side of the body to enhance their level of cooperative communication within the brain. Drawing is a perfect vehicle for this development.

We also talk about the tendencies of each hemisphere with the now classic references of the left brain being more linear and logical and the right being more spatial and spontaneous. This means the right brain is more aware of the big picture and can make connections within that expanded perspective. The left brain is better at focusing in and finding an optimal and logical pathway from here to there within that big picture.

Norman Rockwell's traditional, realistic Americana scenes on the cover of Saturday Evening Post – as seen in his classic *The Runaway* – are a great example of left-brain art. Another example is Andrew Wyeth's realistic and highly detailed painting, *Christine's World*. The earth tones of the painting and the subject matter and the style are both quite realistic, with seemingly each blade of grass in the field being individually painted. The left brain does love detail.

Right-brain art is going to use more primary colors and have perhaps a fantasy or dream-like feel to it. While many of Marc Chagall's paintings would be in that style, *The Blue Circus* with a fish and a woman floating randomly in the air, using blue, red and a dash of yellow primary colors works as a good example of a right-brain creation. Paul Klee's *Fish Magic* or *Senecio* are also good images of right-brain art.

When I was teaching in Switzerland, I stumbled onto an interesting blend of right and left-brain design, in the Fraumunster Church just off Bahnhof Strasse in Zurich. This 13th century church is quite stately and precise, but the stained-glass windows display the whimsical designs of Chagall.

The Living Camera:

When I talk about the right brain having a big picture perspective and the left brain being more linear and detailed, a good, yet extreme example is the story of an Englishman named Stephan Wiltshire. Stephan is an autistic savant who is known as "The Living Camera" due to his amazing ability to look at and then draw from memory buildings and even entire cities that he's seen from an aerial view.

You may have seen the YouTube video of Stephan where, on his first visit to Rome, he is taken for a 45-minute helicopter ride over the city. He is then given a five-and-a-half-yard wide canvas and three days to draw Rome from his memory of the aerial ride. You can watch how Stephan is able to quite accurately draw the Pantheon with the correct number of columns, the church of St Peters, and the coliseum in such detail that the narrator calls it "A blueprint of reality." When Stephan is complete at the end of the third day, he has drawn the entire city laid out, not only relationally accurate, but with the correct number of windows in all of the main buildings. As his sister shares, "If he'd had more time, he could have filled in more detail."

I believe that our brains also have this innate capability. But with all the busy-ness that is also going on in our brains, we are not as singularly focused and able to hold onto this level of detail and specificity. Stephan is indeed showing us how amazing our untapped capabilities can be.

The integrative process I've used with my clients involves having people begin by drawing relatively simple objects. (A candlestick or a myriad of other options were available.) I'd have them first use one hand and then the other to draw the object. The challenge I'd give them, though, is that they could not lift their pen off the paper, so the image is done in one continuous line (left brain).

The other little challenge in this learning exercise was that, wherever their eye was looking at on the object, is exactly where their pen needed to be in the drawing. So, wherever they were looking at a shadow or a curve, their eyes were looking at the same place the pen was drawing. They were also supported, especially in the beginning, to keep their eye and pen moving in sync with each other. In other words, no stopping to look anywhere other than where you were drawing. Oh, and they also couldn't look down at what they were drawing. Almost all of the participants were non-artists, so doing this without even looking, at first seemed a little over-the-top uncomfortable.

So, while the right brain delighted in holding the big picture of the object being drawn, with an awareness of the subtlest of changes in light and texture, the left brain felt comfortable with the focus and the linear continuous line. What the more left-brain people didn't like was not being able to look at the drawing. It drove them nuts. People who are generally more predominately left brain, like engineers, lawyers, and other logical, linear careers, had to learn to trust their right brain to do a job that their left brain didn't understand. It's kind of like Alan, the high-powered attorney that Tim Gallwey was working with on his tennis serve. He didn't understand how his right brain could so powerfully and accurately place the ball, so he abandoned that skill for his more comfortable and familiar left-brain lob.

After a while, as the two hemispheres began to work more comfortably together, the blooming artists were allowed to look at the drawing 10% of the time, just glancing down at the image from time to time. To their amazement, they'd realize that not only did the object look like what they were drawing, but that they were often the same exact size. In other words, they could take the candlestick (or whatever the object was) and lay it on its side on top of the drawing, and, thanks to the right brain's spatial awareness, they were mirror images. By the end of the weekend, each of the participant's left and right brains were getting along quite well and having a delightful time. The before and after shows were always a hit.

For those more adventuresome types, there was a third day in which we got into drawing faces. Just as I had been when I first did this work, all of the participants were blown away as we observed the magnitude of the artist's awareness that was revealed in their drawings. For instance, you could easily see when the model was looking outwardly as one side of their face was being drawn, and when the model was looking thoughtfully inward when the other side was being drawn. You could actually discern this difference in the drawing of the model's eyes. With the right brain's big-picture awareness and the left brain's ability to capture detail, some very lovely and captivating drawings emerged.

All of this drawing was interspersed with information about the innate abilities of the two hemispheres of the neocortex, the emotional limbic brain, the brainstem and the cerebellum. The cerebellum, as it turns out, is much more than just the seat of muscle memory. New research shows that it deeply influences thoughts and emotions. It fine-tunes cognitive function in a similar way to how it fine-tunes motor movement. It's also where the more deep-seated subconscious memories are held.

A way to think about how our brains function is that the thinking brain – which is the right and left sides of the neocortex – takes in and processes information, deciding amongst other things how we should most reasonably react to what our senses bring in. The frontal lobe, which is a part of the neocortex, has the role of the brain's CEO in this mental process.

As the neocortex processes input, it will be considering if we should use established patterns and reactions or perhaps even change our behavior as a result of the information being received. It will also be sending chemical signals to the limbic brain, which is tucked in just beneath the neocortex.

The limbic brain is often referred to as the mammalian, or emotional brain. As the limbic, or feeling brain, receives the neocortex's chemical signals, it interprets them and sends them out as chemical and emotional signals to the body. These signals result in your emotional and even physical reactions to the information. In this process, the limbic brain (along with the brainstem) is also helping us to form long-term memories. When the neocortex takes in information that seems similar to a past experience, the limbic brain will send out related emotions that help us remember and react accordingly to that event.

The greater the emotional charge around a memory, the greater our memory of the event tends to be.

The limbic system and the brainstem operate constantly, solving complex problems without any conscious effort. In upgrading our old programming and integrating the whole brain, they play a big role in our becoming comfortable with and being able to supportively use all of our emotions. They also are key players in forging new habits. When you have a gut feeling that something is wrong, it is because your emotional brain has identified a problem that is perhaps invisible to your thinking brain.

The limbic brain is also in chemical or neurological communication with the cerebellum, which is located towards the back and at the base of the brain. As the cerebellum receives highly charged or repeatedly seen information, it can take those experiences and long-term memories and makes them part of your subconscious programming. The cerebellum is often times still referred to as the reptilian brain, as it will trigger deeply entrenched reactive patterns.

These reactive patterns can be seen when someone emotionally snaps and unconsciously reacts to a situation that triggers a subconscious memory. You can see it with military personnel who have suffered from PTSD when there is a loud bang or if they are grabbed or even touched in the wrong way.

Here's how this science rolled into my five-step process benefits you: As we breathe into and clear up our unsupportive subconscious neurological brain patterns and integrate our whole brain, the brain becomes quieter and more present with what is actually going on in the here and now. The present is made up from our past and future, so the less we are distracted by the past or worried about the future, the more in that present moment we are able to be. That quiet and present place lets us optimize how we use the amount of time we have. If, for example, your partner wants a more deeply connected relationship and more quality time, what they are really asking for is for you to be more present with them. In the present, you will be more aware of what they are saying, feeling, needing, and wanting from or with you. So, while it might seem like they are wanting more time, what they are really asking for is more of you, which you can only give them if you are more present. Again, it's not a time problem, but a matter of what you are doing or not doing with the time that you're with them.

A personal and recent example of this brain integration-in-action is when I started taking Tai-Kwon-Do. For the first month or so, it was a truly humbling experience as I tried to recall and perform the moves that I had been working on. But, as my thinking brain (the neocortex) started to better connect with my feeling brain (the limbic brain), I was able experience my mind and body working more closely together as one. You know how when you try something new, you can be "up in your head" trying to figure it out? Well, as your limbic brain repeatedly experiences those movement patterns, it begins to more fully participate and, over time, you find a supportive balance between that thinking and feeling (body oriented) brain. With years of repeating those movements, a person will find the cerebellum comes into play so that the repetitive movements and behaviors become automatic. They are beyond having to think about it or to rely on just the body's memory of it. The movement or form has become an innate program that is memorized in their subconscious. We call that "being in the flow."

Having rewritten your program for getting love to one of accepting and loving yourself, you've already begun the process of neurologically rewiring our brain. Just as you'll use the breath to breathe yourself down into your cave where you can discover the source of your challenges, you can now use your breathing to help you open up the chemical gateways and integrate the whole brain. You can then be working smarter, and getting things done more effectively in less time. You will naturally abandon activities that are not in alignment with your highest intention, which you are now able to stay fully focused on. This, of course, gives you more time to be doing the things that best support you.

In step one of the 5 Steps of Personal Evolution process, you are breathing within and becoming aware of your long-term and subconscious memories. As you breathe into and fully acknowledge, express, and release the emotions around those memories, you cut your emotional attachment to continuing to fire and wire those old, unsupportive, brain patterns. Your past is still your past, but you are no longer at the effect of it. The anchor line has been cut and you are free to sail off into your life.

Each of these five steps are intertwined and are always working together. In this case, the healing that you are breathing into in step one is also laying the groundwork for the brain integration process of step three. In step one of this five step process, you are clearing your attachments to and the wiring of those past experiences. This prepares and opens the mind to the new firing and rewiring that takes place in the third step of integrating and using your whole brain.

As you begin to more fully introduce and use the two hemispheres of the neocortex (left and right brains) as a team, they begin to trust and rely on each other's skills and innate abilities to greatly enhance your thinking abilities. But, while you're rewiring the left and right brain, you're also affecting those old tracks that have been woven within the "we" and "I" (mammalian and reptilian) brain's neurological patterns. You then start to break down those old "wired together" tracks. You start paying attention to how your dominant brain pattern affects and is reflected in your thinking, dressing, speaking, eating, career choice, how you do your work, your social connections, and – truly – nearly all aspects of your life.

As you become aware of your old patterns, you begin to see where they have been limiting you and how you might choose to retrain your brain into continuing to develop as an integrated whole. Integrating your brain allows you to literally declutter your brain so there is less noise and less distraction, which results in greater focus and the ability to be present with what you are doing. You have more resources and creative genius available to you for your project at hand. All of this allows you to use your time more efficiently and effectively, which results in additional time to invest in whatever is most important to you.

Keep in mind that the strength of those old thoughts and neurological patterns was established in relationship to the emotional levels that you were then experiencing. Strong emotion acts as the "install" button to our brain's wiring patterns. It works this way whether the emotions are positive or negative. So, the more highly emotionally charged your new experiences are, the more set the upgraded wiring and memories will become. Those events that occurred in your childhood were emotionally charged enough that you weren't able to process and move beyond them back then as a child. This resulted in a part of you getting stuck back there and that part being left behind.

While there were, no doubt, many emotions involved, fear was certainly a big player. Just as that fear held you in the past, so I'd recommend we use very engaged emotions of forgiveness, appreciation, understanding, and especially your love to secure your new memories and brain patterns in place. Joy, excitement, and giggling can also work well for added emphasis and deeper re-patterning.

Just as you needed to acknowledge, express, and let go of the old emotional programming to heal, you can now fully acknowledge, express, and embrace your new feelings of love, joy, and compassion to establish your new memories and emotional references as the foundation of your upgraded life.

We'll also explore how your being emotionally clear, able to breathe into your depths within, and having an integrated whole brain will give you full access to your prefrontal cortex – the CEO of your brain. I hope you are beginning to see how, with the amazing plasticity of the brain, you are literally able to consciously neurologically rewire your old patterns in new ways that better support you. This allows you to move beyond being at the effect of the past or your current stumbling blocks and enjoy living more and more fully and creatively in the present. From there, you get to choose the future you wish to live.

Chapter 7

Step 4: Mindfulness and the New Mind

"To enjoy good health, to bring true happiness to one's family, to bring peace to all, one must first discipline and control one's own mind. If a man can control his mind, he can find the way to Enlightenment, and all wisdom and virtue will naturally come to him."
–Buddha

While each step of this evolutionary process relies on and overlaps the others, mindfulness is certainly at the heart of your personal development upgrade. Whether you are currently engulfed in the daily dramas of your business, or more in a state of being and living in the present, mindfulness is the key to your shifting to the next level. While the "next level" is different for each of us, your next level will look like you having a quieter, more efficient and effective mind. You will be more aware and function from and with a higher degree of consciousness which means your entire perspective and experience of life will be enhanced. What you focus on will be what you are creating. What you are thinking about, paying attention to, fearing, or desiring, will be what develops in your life. Fortunately, as we've talked about before, you will also become clearer and more focused on your highest intention, yet with access to even more innate ability to fulfill it. So, whatever it is you are creating will unfold from that intention. I know your intention will be a supportive one for yourself and others, and you can trust that all that comes into your life is a perfect gift to support you on your journey. Really.

> *"The present is made up of material called the past and the future, and the past and the future are here in what we call the present."*
> –Thich Nhat Hanh

Mindfulness is giving our attention to something; it is what brings us back to being present. It is being aware of the bigger picture, yet able to focus on where we are and what's going on in the very moment. For mindfulness to support us on our journey, we will develop a type of mindfulness where we are open and curious about what comes into our life – whether from the outside, or arising from within. In this kind of mindful, curious state, we accept everything without judgment, and without reacting to it.

In step one, we explored healing your emotional backlog, rewriting your core program (your program for getting love), and learning to look within for self-acceptance and answers to our life's questions. Looking deeply into the past allows us to learn things that can benefit the present and the future. With that revised and enhanced foundation in place, you are able to breathe more fully and deeply into the depths and the expansiveness of who you truly are (step two). These first two steps help you integrate and use your whole brain on an entirely new level. With the integration of your neocortex, limbic system, and cerebellum, you have connected your thoughts to your emotions and your mind to your body, which allows you to more consistently choose and change your state of being. With you in charge as the CEO, you have become a competent and aware, proactive creator of your life. Mindfulness accelerates, deepens, and supports your shift into a higher state of being and functioning in the world.

Most people find they become attached to – and live out their lives in – a comfort zone of their own creation. Since change is the one constant of life, those comfort zones are generally not a fixed point but involve a range of consciousness and awareness. If we create an arbitrary scale with "1" being a lower state of consciousness and "100" being a fully conscious being, some people might enjoy the range between 18 and 27, while others find 36 to 41 most comfy. Since our level of consciousness determines how we see and experience reality, each range will have a different set of challenges and opportunities. That old saying, "We never get more than we can handle," is true because we are the ones ultimately choosing what we allow ourselves to see, what we take on, and what we're willing to deal with. We choose our own level of growth and awareness. The speed and timing of our expansion is up to us.

It's easy to become aware of the range of our comfort zone, as when we deviate too far outside of it, we unconsciously behave in a way that brings us right back in. If things get too bad, we may do whatever we can to pull ourselves together and raise our level of consciousness so that life is more stable. We might eat better, start exercising, focus on resolving a drama going on in our life, or begin meditating again. Similarly, if we start to expand our consciousness beyond our comfort range, then we often find ourselves doing whatever it is that we like to do to lower our consciousness. Alcohol, for example, is a great tool for helping lower our awareness and helping us deny and control our emotional backlog. We can also contract back down into our comfort zone by starting to focus more on the problems in our life, or we can start hanging out with people or in places that support a lower level of awareness. A favorite for many is to just start eating more and eating less consciously. They all can do the job. A classic example that many of us are familiar with is when people go to a workshop or have a personal growth experience that results in their feeling expanded and wonderful. They feel like they've got it all figured out and are on top of the world. The problem is, that within a couple of weeks, they find they've reverted right back into the familiar range of their former comfort zone. While we fully intended to expand, we got sucked right back by our old thinking, habits, and patterns without hardly noticing it.

What brings people back down from those temporary highs is all of their ways of being that are a part of their emotional backlog and program for trying to get love from outside of themselves. It's the rubber band effect that unfortunately can also make people feel that there is something wrong with them, because they can't seem to make the changes that their trusted thought leaders tell them are so easy to make.

If you haven't done the deeper emotional clearing and foundational work, whatever you create going forward is at risk of tumbling down – especially when you run into a particularly difficult period or a challenge in your life. And, yes, running into challenges is part of the journey, but with this overall process, those challenges become very real and even appreciated opportunities.

When we have a life-quake:

I was talking with a highly ranked master in the martial arts, and he was sharing with me that it felt like some challenges in his primary relationship were throwing him off. In his art, Rick had literally become a master of taking an opponent's energy and redirecting it in either a defensive or offensive way. While being highly skilled at redirecting energy in many aspects of his life, Rick still had well-entrenched, reactive emotional buttons that had been there since childhood. As is the case for most of us, our spouse can push our buttons like nobody else. When this happened between Rick and his wife, he was caught off guard and felt like he'd been kicked in the gut. In spite of all of the amazing personal growth work he had done in his life, there were still some old emotional patterns in place, and now bubbling up for him to acknowledge and heal.

Sure enough, as Rick began to breathe and explore his inner cave in our work together, he could feel where his breath caught and tears began to well up in his eyes. As Rick continued to look deeper, we were able to clearly see the source of the emotion that was troubling him. It turns out that as a kid growing up within his family, it was not at all okay for him to express anger. Rick recognized that the same dynamic was being played out in his own relationship with his wife. His concern was, that if he brought up difficult topics he wanted to discuss, his wife would get angry. As a kid, we might logically feel that if we make our "significant others" (our caretakers – usually Mom or Dad) angry enough, that they might leave. This would, of course, be devastating for a child. But here Rick realized that he was at the effect of that old, unhealed, emotional thread. Once he did the work of acknowledging, expressing, and releasing that old, unhealed, emotional backlog, Rick was able to more comfortably and confidently connect and communicate with his wife. This is true for everyone – the more in touch and comfortable we are with ourselves, the more fully we show up with and for others in our life.

Not surprisingly, I have watched Rick over the past couple of years growing in many areas of his life, and literally taking his life up to the next level. The great thing is, Rick is paying it forward in a big way. He is taking his whole dojo community up several notches, and I'm hoping that influence will reach into and throughout the entire U.S. martial-arts community as well. It is so much fun and so rewarding to watch.

One of Rick's favorite stories is of an old samurai named Miyamoto Musashi who was the top swordsman in Japan. As the accomplished samurai got older, he began using his highly focused mind and skills in calligraphy. Like in the old west where the top gun slinger would be challenged by the young bucks who were trying to make a name for themselves, so it was in old Japan. Skilled swordsmen from the

Miyamoto Musashi
Self-portrait, Samurai

Calligraphy
by Musashi

different schools would journey to the master's hilltop retreat and challenge him to a fight. Having exchanged the sword for the calligraphy brush, the master would only use a stick to fend off the pesky challenger. With his many decades of training his mind and body, the old sword master had learned to live his life consciously in the present moment. From this expanded, aware state, it was as if his young challengers were moving in slow motion.

Musashi was the author of *The Book of Five Rings*, which is about the strategy, techniques, and philosophy of sword fighting. His mastery of being mindful and present was evidenced by his skills with the sword, but, as he also shared, "When I apply the principles of strategy to the ways of different arts and crafts, I no longer have need for a teacher in any domain."

Being present and focused are at the heart of being mindful, and are key aspects in the art of life. The beauty and depth of Japanese gardens, calligraphy, and many of the ancient arts came from those old samurai who had elevated their ability to live mindfully in all areas of their lives. I see Rick's path clearly leading in that direction.

It is in seeing our challenges as opportunities to grow, and being willing to go even more deeply within to heal, that we begin to appreciate and trust the perfection of the universe. We begin to trust that whatever is coming to us in our life is a gift that is perfectly designed to support us in opening up our hearts and loving more fully. We begin to realize and gratefully embrace that we do live in abundance, and that feelings of scarcity can only come out of our fears and unresolved emotional issues from the past.

> *"We can correct the past. The past is here; and if we get deeply in touch with the present, we can touch the past as well, and transform it."*
> –Thich Nhat Hanh

Time to what?

When we feel like we don't have enough time for important things like taking care of ourselves, our primary relationship, and pet projects that will require us to play on a higher level, it's easier to look outside of ourselves for what needs adjusting. But, the truth is, as you've been seeing, the real adjustments need to be made within. Focusing on the outer aspects of your life validates who you have become. It's even easy and alluring to take on workaholic qualities as you try to juggle all of your successful and impactful projects. While at times a little overwhelming, it still feels comfortable and safe, even validating, to keep doing and being what you know – what you trust.

The problem is that you can only busy yourself so much before the avalanche of your success catches up with you and sweeps you away – away from being able to look deeper within, being able to more deeply connect with your partner, or taking better care of yourself. That lack of time due to your success also distracts you from looking deeper within and recognizing the real reason that you're not getting that book or special project done. Perhaps you know, deep down, that you will have to change to get it done. You know that you will have to shift gears and play on a more conscious and expanded level. Your lack of time may actually be just a symptom of a deeper challenge. Perhaps you didn't know how to meet that challenge before. Now you do. Consider whether you may be experiencing resistance to going into that deep-down place that would allow you to take yourself and your work up to the next level.

I'd like you to consider whether that inner shift – which is the main subject of this book – may be the real answer to your challenge at hand. That inner shift is what will give you the quality time, higher focus, and expanded perspective that you need in order to take better care of yourself, love more deeply, and create greater and ever-more rewarding results in your life and work. Again, I recognize you are a successful leader and a guide in many ways. With all due respect, I am now only suggesting that symptoms, like "not having enough time" and other challenges in our lives, often are the very indicators I referred to earlier. It is important that we are mindful enough to welcome those indicators and respond to them by going even more deeply within than we have before. There is, as you are fully aware, always another level of letting go and becoming.

Gifts from a mindful meditation:

Years ago, I was out on a rugged point just below Big Sur. I had been going there for years and knew the area well. I'd taken the long walk out to the far end of the point just as the sun was setting. After enjoying a splendiferous night of meditation, I had just started back along the main path where I could hear the surf breaking along the cliffs of the rugged coastline about fifteen yards off to my right. It was about 1 a.m. and without enough moonlight to see the path, so I turned on my small flashlight. I was walking along, reflecting on what a marvelous evening it had been and how fortunate I was to be there, when my flashlight went out. No biggie, as I always have a spare bulb and batteries. It was too dark to see, but I finally got the batteries changed. Only problem is, the flashlight still wasn't working.

Just as I as I started to change the bulb, there was a sudden, heart-stopping huge crash not fifteen feet to my right. I froze. I'm never much afraid of animals when I'm out in nature, but other people do worry me, and only something as large as a man could have made that sound. I was blind and, even with all of my training, scared shitless. There was no real way to prepare myself for whatever might come at me at any moment, so I instinctively took a knee, closed my eyes, and took several full, deep breaths to find my center again.

When I opened my eyes a moment later, I was as fully present as I'd ever been. In this meta-mindful state, after having been in many hours of meditation, I was amazed to see that all of the plants were glowing. The trees and plants cast so much light that I could now clearly see the path and the area around me. Looking in the direction of the crashing noise, I didn't see anything coming at me, or for that matter, anything at all that could attack me. A part of my logical brain started considering what could have caused that noise, and all it came up with was that perhaps a large limb had fallen from a tree. There was little if any wind, but, as Sherlock Holmes said, "When you have eliminated the impossible, whatever remains, however improbable, must be the truth."

While I'll never know what caused the sound, I will always consider accessing the ability to literally see the light and the life force of the plants, as one of the more delightful gifts life has offered me. Yes, being mindful and present in the moments of your life will offer you exceptional experiences that you'd otherwise never even believe could happen. Mindfulness gives us access to the magic, and the magic comes when we are fully present and at one with the world and the universe. So many incredible experiences await us, and we are so very fortunate to be living and playing in it all.

Benefits of mindfulness:

Rewriting your core program for getting love supports you in shifting from a more fear-based reaction to change in your life, to one of trust and gratitude for the opportunity that change offers us. Even if fear only plays a small part in your life, this shift will still be significant, relevant, and true for you. A shift in your core programming also shifts your perception from one of living your life from a sense of scarcity, to one of experiencing a life of overflowing abundance. You come to welcome change, because you know that it is change that makes transformation possible.

The shift into being grateful for the changes in your life, allows you to relax and be more mindful, which results in your having a quieter mind. With a quieter mind, you'll find yourself breathing more naturally and fully, which sends a message to your brain that you are fine, and not in flight or fight. Your nervous system gets back on track and is again working to support your health and well-being. From this state of being, you will be able to more easily and fully integrate and be able to access your integrated whole brain and all of the innate gifts that are available within it. Along with many other great tools, in a more mindful state, you will be able to access your unlimited imagination and be able to more easily create what you envision. In that mindful place, all of your senses and emotions will tell you when you are taking the most supportive path towards leading a fulfilling, happy, and successful life. You will also have the heightened ability to maintain your undistracted intention and focus, continuing to move along that path to fulfilling your purpose and creating your highest intention.

In my work with clients, we journey deep within to identify the deepest source of their challenges, discomforts, and pain. Once we identify the source, we can also recognize and understand what is causing their suffering or struggle. We can then see what it is that they need to do, so that they can reach the level of health and wellbeing they'd like to experience in their body, mind, and spirit. What is so delightful about mindfulness, is that it allows them to continue to be aware of and make the supportive choices in their life that will bring them the joy, peace, and success that we all seem to long for.

Granted, I have never asked anyone a question to which, with a little breathing and support, they didn't know the answer. But living mindfully helps us to be consciously aware of those answers and the choices we are making. Being mindful also lets us know whether those choices will result in greater suffering or joy. That ability saves people a whole lot of pain and drama. Yet, as you have no doubt witnessed, the last thing that most people want to do is to be aware and have to take full responsibility for their life. But you're not "most people." You are a leader, and you look for opportunities to be consciously creating your life and supporting others in doing the same. You understand that the more mindful we are, the more mindful our friends, community, nation, and world will be. You are doing your very best to "be the change that you wish to see."

As Thich Nhat Hahn shares, "With mindful breathing, mindful being, and mindful living, we can overcome our fears, despair, anger, and longing." This is the level that you are perhaps being called to play on, even more fully than you already are.

In a mindful present moment, we are in a place of openness and curiosity, accepting what we experience without reacting or judging. We are looking for the gift rather than shrinking back from something we're prejudging as a threat to our comfort zone.

That is one of the many benefits of having gone back into your cave and done the emotional healing needed so that your emotions can be in alignment with the fully integrated, whole-brain-generated, creative thoughts that your quiet mind is focused on. Since everything is made up of energy, you now have all of the energy of your emotions and thoughts, body and mind in sync, clearly communicating your intention for the future that you'd like to create.

This conscious way of being, thinking, and acting becomes a finely-tuned way of life. As you unify your thoughts and emotions, and are living in the present, you will be continually upgrading your core program (and your life). When you notice your breath catching, or an emotion being triggered by a thought, or something going on in your life, rather than contract with fear, you will instead be able to comfortably breathe into and through whatever it is you're bumping up against. You don't have to intentionally create and maintain boundaries, because they will naturally evolve as a result of how you are consciously living your life. There's no reason to do the work of acknowledging, expressing, and releasing your old emotional backlog if you're just going to create a new backlog! Open the gates and turn on the lights in your cave, so that you are mindful of whatever comes into your life. You can then deal with it in the present moment in a supportive way. Redecorate and have a party so that others, like your partner and close friends, know they are welcome into your heart and into your cave.

You can pay it all forward by making sure to encourage your tribe or community to support each other in seeing what's not working so well, as well as what is. You are the "safe-space-maker" and guide, so that your students and clients can be the "growth-risk-takers." This is your opportunity to lead by example in a small way that makes a big difference.

Having done the work, you get to develop a conscious relationship with yourself and others that is about healing and being emotionally honest – one in which there are no taboo topics or areas that are too sensitive or too uncomfortable to talk about. You'll find yourself being present and curious, without fear and judgment. You'll more naturally let yourself out and others in. Like others who have taken this path, you'll find that as you take better care of yourself, you'll be happier and more creative and efficient, making better use of your time. The more focused you are on your highest priorities, the less side-tracked you'll become. I know you're doing a lot of great things, but are you doing the great things that you really want to be doing? As the weathered yellow sticky note on my computer says, "Quiet mind – happy life."

Everything relates to mindfulness and mindfulness relates to everything. Being mindful will allow you to take better care of yourself and have more time to do what you truly want to do. This five-step evolutionary process will take you into that deeper level of mindfulness that can become your way of life.

Pathways of mindfulness:

I'm sure that you've witnessed the flood of mindfulness information entering the mainstream via books and workshops. There was a program on PBS recently called *Mindfulness Goes Mainstream* where they show how mindfulness programs are being used in both academic and business settings. I remember that for my first PhD proposal that involved brain integration and mindfulness, my professors at UCSB said it was just too far out. I guess "far out" is the new "in."

So, while I appreciate that there is a lot of information out there, I'll just be sharing some mindful practices that I have found invaluable on my journey.

You might have gotten the impression, somewhere along the line here, that I feel that the breath is a vital tool on the path. I know I've been subtle about it, but perhaps it caught your attention. My students in Switzerland used to jokingly tell new people coming to a meditation or a workshop that, "If you don't understand what he said, he probably just said, 'Breathe.'" I'll admit, I'm a big fan of breathing and the absolute magic that it has created in my life.

So, what I'd like to share with you now is how you can use your breathing to bring you back into and maintain a mindful state. While there are yantras, mantras, and a hundred other tools out there to use as your focus, the breath is always right there and fully available for you to use at any and all times. Since how you are breathing largely determines your state of consciousness, you can choose both your state of consciousness and level of mindfulness by how you breathe.

After having done the work described in chapters four, five, and six, you will find that you are able to maintain a normal and relaxed, yet full breathing pattern for much of your life. As you are sitting and reading, talking, walking, or working, you will feel your belly expand out and then relatively flatten a bit with each breath. Even during events that might have earlier caused you to stop breathing and to literally hold your breath, you may now find yourself just shifting how you breathe, so that you can stay curious and mindful.

Keep in mind that, when you do find it difficult to move back into and maintain your breath, it is a huge indicator that you are bumping up against something that, on some level, you are finding uncomfortable. These are the places where other people usually stop breathing, because they either don't know how or don't feel comfortable processing and breathing into, healing, and moving through those challenges and the emotions that may be involved. It is when they stop breathing that they are stuffing down their emotions around the issue, and that is how that area of their life gets stuck. This is exactly how we created our emotional backlog in the first place. As children, we had few other options, but now we know better. As we saw in chapter four, the amount of energy that people end up using to maintain and suppress that emotional backlog significantly drains them of their personal power, as well as their ability to stay present and mindfully create their life.

I have a friend who pokes me by saying something like, "Oh, you're always processing something." In a sense, he is right. I am mindfully breathing into whatever is coming into my life in that present moment and seeing how this too is an opportunity to grow. I call this being mindful and present, and it keeps my life moving along quite well.

I was just remembering when my dad would sit me down when he was upset with me and wanted to "talk" about it. This meant he talked, and I was supposed to listen. What often happened though, was that he would get even more upset because I'd be breathing deeply. Frustrated, he'd tell me to, "Quit breathing like that!" As a kid, well under age ten or twelve, I, of course, didn't have any idea what he was talking about, but it seems this breathing interest of mine has been around for quite a while.

I'm an avid gardener and one thing that I'm regularly telling people is that plants don't just suddenly die. There are generally plenty of indicators (unless they've been sprayed with weed killer) that they're in stress, if you're paying any attention at all. People are essentially the same. So, the sooner you can recognize that you're bumping up against something, the better. If you're like most of us, there are indicators in your body when you're feeling stressed. For me, my breath gets shallower, then my jaw tightens, and, if I ignore it, my back starts to get tight and sore. For others, it could be their neck, or their stomach, or headaches, or hunger. It really doesn't matter what the signal is, just that you begin to recognize it and use the breath to bring you back to a more mindful, curious, and supportive state. The earlier you can notice the subtlest of the indicators, the more easily you can remember to breathe and get re-centered. It is the difference of changing the pathway of a trickling stream, or trying to change that of a raging river.

So, it just doesn't matter where you are or what is going on, you still want to be mindful and present. If you're in a bank line and realizing its's going to make you late for your next appointment, breathe. Yes, just breathe. It's like doing the STOP process that we went over in chapter five. You take a moment to relax or stop, then take in several gentle deep breaths. As you are breathing, take a look within and observe how you are feeling and what you need. Breathe and let yourself see what your best next step is in that moment. Then proceed, taking action. This brings you back into a mindful state.

Now, continue to breathe and be curious; breathe and non-judgmentally look at the situation and take your best next step, and then your next and so on. If you can't find your breath, then focus on your body and consciously take in several full deep breaths. It will come, just trust and breathe.

"How do I remain mindful amidst all the dramas and traumas, life-quakes, and deadlines?" you might ask. Let your breath be your focus and your guide. The degree that you are getting plugged in by something is the degree that you will have difficulty breathing. If it's just a little thing, then just taking a normal breath will bring you back. If it's someone doing something that violates your images and expectation of how people should behave, then you will need to breathe more deeply and fully. If you're faced with a trauma or tragedy, then an emotional release is necessary to help get your emotions out so you can fully breathe again.

So, let's make a breathing calibration scale (1-10), with one being a mild distraction and ten being a traumatic event. This will give you a pretty good sense of how to keep yourself clear and open to being mindful in any type of situation.

1. With a scale one event, just remember to breathe and then breathe again…

2. With a scale two event, take in a breath and slowly let it out, again and then yet again…

3. With an event at a three, breathe in and slowly exhale through your slightly open mouth, and then continue…

4. With an event of four on the scale, breathe in and, as you subtly constrict your throat, slowly extend your exhale. You will hear the air moving through the subtly constricted area. Stay with this until you can relax and breathe normally.

5. At this level of a five event, repeat what you were doing in a four, but with every other breath, inhale and then release two quick bursts of exhale out of your nose. Then go back into level four breathing…

6. An event on a scale of six, breathe in and make an extended vowel sound like "ooooo…" or "ah…" (It doesn't have to be loud but go with what feels right.) I guess, if it gets really scary you could switch to an "eeeee…," but other people might notice. Your call. Stay with this until you can do level five, and then get back to level four and so on.…

7. With an event on a scale of seven, take in a full deep breath and just let it go, repeat several times, and then move into the directions for a six and then keep going down this scale of response until you are present and mindful again.

8. On a scale of eight, you are possibly going to have to be moving your body and making a sound until you can get back down to and follow the directions for a seven. This will allow you to move and release more energy. Breathe your way back down the scale as you settle down.

9. On a level of nine, it would be best to find support from another person and be acknowledging and expressing your feelings. If it isn't appropriate to express your emotions at the time, like in a family tragedy or a war situation, then make sure to fully attend to yourself as soon as you can. Breathe into and through this as fully as you can, so you don't create new backlog.

10. A level of ten is a life-quake, and all you can do is trust and let go. Breathe fully and deeply when you can, as much as you can. Life comes to us in waves, so just focus on getting through each wave. Let a part of you remember that the more difficult the challenge,

the more rewarding the healing can be. Without trying to regulate and control your emotions, let whatever feelings want to come up, come up. It's totally appropriate here to seek out as much help as you need, for as long as you need it.

My point is that it just doesn't matter what it is you are facing and dealing with in life, there is the opportunity to let go of old emotional backlog that's finding its way out, and to breathe and remember to bring yourself back to a present and mindful state. From there, you will have the most aware and supportive perspective. You will also be able to see and take action on whatever your best, next-available step may be. Life is a process. Breathing and being mindful is what helps you through any and all aspects of that process. I am intimately familiar with all of these stages on the scale, and because of that, I'm still here and thriving.

The ins and outs of mindfulness:

Thich Nhat Hanh has a favorite method for being mindful that also involves the breath. Since he is a Zen monk, it's not too surprising that the method is delightful in its simplicity and yet very powerful in creating results. You have likely heard of it, if not used it yourself. He is certainly a master, and if it works for him, we may want to at least give it a look.

He uses this method in both his sitting and walking meditations, so you could find it useful in many different circumstances. As you are sitting, during and with each inhale, inwardly say "in." The next thing that you do is, during and with each exhale, inwardly say, "out." In and out, during and with each breath, again and again, until you find that place of silence within where there is no more in or out, or an awareness of a you to say it. You can, of course, bring yourself back with the "ins" and "outs" of your breath at any time you wish.

The walking meditation gets a lot more complicated (that's a joke) as during one step you inhale, silently saying "in," during and with each inhale, and then during the next step, you exhale, silently saying "out," during and with that exhale, and each exhale thereafter. There you've got it. The tricky part is that you get to decide how many steps you want to take in between your inhale and exhale. It could be every step, if they are slow and consciously taken, or you may enjoy a faster pace, taking three steps during and with each breath. I regularly enjoy using this method on my beach walks, and it is really quite a beautiful experience. I recommend that you explore and play with these ideas, modifying them to suit your temperament and needs.

I wish you a mindful day, and a mindful life, filled with presence.

Chapter 8

Step 5: Access and Live from Big Mind

"To the mind that is still, the whole universe surrenders."
—Lao Tzu

I was on stage helping Buckminster Fuller in one of his classic presentations about *Spaceship Earth* and how, if run properly, the planet could take good care of us all. I was in my late twenties and thrilled to be getting to know and work with Bucky. Little did I realize how profoundly he was influencing me.

The presentation was going along well when, in the middle of an idea he was sharing, he just stopped. As I watched him, I could see that his eyes were looking up. As suddenly as he had stopped, within a short time he started back up again. After the presentation, I asked him what he was doing in that extended moment, and he casually said, "Waiting for information." My questioning look prompted him to share how he would often just stop and wait in the silence for the right information to come in.

I had been meditating for years, so I understood quieting my mind, but Bucky opened a doorway from that place of silence into the Universal Library, where all of the answers can be found. As I learned from that exchange, I didn't have to know everything; all I had to do was use my library card of silence to access and download the most viable information needed in the moment.

We can often times feel like trying harder, doing more (efforting), and staying busy are what we need to do to get things done. These are common beliefs we picked up from our parents and society as a whole, and we continue to honor them all by adopting these limiting beliefs for ourselves. These attitudes, beliefs, and unconscious motivations are really just a part of our program for getting acceptance and love. While we might be unconsciously validating our life by staying busy or being a workaholic, it doesn't mean we are working as effectively as we could and accomplishing those things that we most value.

It's like people who say they don't have time to sit and meditate for twenty minutes and then spend all day running in circles and having to redo much of the work that they just did. Life and work done from a conscious and mindful place is far more productive that just being distractedly busy day after day.

I can only imagine that your success is largely due to your ability to stay focused and get projects done. And I trust that you have accomplished a great deal in your life. But taking a moment and shifting your consciousness into a quieter place where you can access this higher mind – or Big Mind, as I call it – can not only save you hours, but days, months, and even years of work. From your Big Mind perspective, you more clearly see what you want to do, how you can most effectively do it, and what the results of the project will be. With Big Mind, you don't have to explore all of the dead ends of the labyrinth. Instead, you are able to see and enjoy walking the clear path through it, right to your destination.

As my life has unfolded, I've found numerous uses for this handy skill of accessing the Universal Library. When I first started seeing counseling clients, I noticed that my old rescuer mode would kick in, as I was attached to images and expectations of how I would help them. Of course, these images and expectations only kept me from breathing and being present, so that wasn't going to work. I soon learned to trust that, as I sat in the silence, whatever was the very best and most supportive thing for me to say or do would come in. It was very effective, but a little baffling at first, as I was basically being paid to do nothing. Yet it was clearly the most supportive way to serve my clients.

As it turned out, quieting my mind and getting out of the way was perhaps my best skill. I gave a lot of public talks and meditations in Europe and the US and seldom had more than a quickly scribbled mind map to go from. Especially during the Q & A, my ability to go into, what by that time I referred to as *Big Mind*, was invaluable. All I had to do was breathe, be present in the silence, and watch what came out. By that time, much of my work was based on really doing nothing; that is, nothing but sitting in the silence or accessing, downloading, and sharing Big Mind images, guidance, and information.

I earlier shared that I am an avid gardener, but the truth is, as I taught in Europe and traveled and studied throughout the world, quite often I used my time off to wander about in nature and to study various gardens. My interest and studies in Buddhism took me to Japan, where I could meditate for hours in breath-giving settings. I had created a Japanese garden in my front yard and, through the years, had been asked to design and built several others by fans of the art.

A wealthy dot-com couple approached me and wanted me to design and build a large Japanese garden on an acre of their estate property that was shaped somewhat like a large bowl. In all honesty, the scale of it was at first intimidating, so I did what I always do when I run into resistance. I went up on the hill behind our home, sat on an old driftwood bench, and meditated. In the beginning, all I did was breathe into my meditation and quiet my mind. As I settled in, I began to focus on the couple – who they were and what they wanted. Then I brought in a vision of the space in which they wanted me to create. This was my canvas.

Over the next two hours, I watched as *Big Mind* filled in the space with a 110' creek meandering down the hillside into a large, organically-shaped 55'x65' pond, complete with a turtle island graced with a magnificent black pine. A bamboo grove filled the far end, serving as a serene backdrop for when the couple was meditating in the teahouse. Giant boulders pulled the theme together, anchoring the space with their strength and texture. Two pathways led down to this magical space, over the arching bridge and around the pond. The bamboo swayed and delicate Japanese maple leaves danced in the gentle breezes. All kinds of birds came and went to the pond. I saw them contentedly bathing and listened as they sang their sweet melodies accompanied by the background symphony of water cascading down the falls. The intoxicating scent of jasmine wafted through the teahouse as the afternoon sun warmed the earth. It was all quite divine.

There were no real drawings needed of the garden because this detailed vision was still in my head. Three months later, the garden was complete. It continues to mature and evolve into the vision that I saw that quiet day on the hill. Once again, I can't really take much credit for it because all I had to do was get out of the way and watch it come together. In talking with the owner a few years later, she said, "You just have to come and see it." While I appreciated her enthusiasm, what she didn't quite get was that I already had seen it, year by year as it would mature, even before it was started.

With full access to universal imagination, *Big Mind* has an unmatched level of creativity that can be used throughout your work and life. It will save you years of time and millions of dollars as you are offered gifts from *Big Mind* that allow you to create your masterpiece. Everything you need is right there for you. You can easily take care of your life's most important needs and wants.

I believed Joseph Campbell when he essentially told me that "The treasures I was seeking could be found within the cave I feared to enter," but I sure never realized that by going through that cave, I'd find the ultimate treasures of *Big Mind*. Keep in mind that *Big Mind* isn't something that is separate from you; it is a part of you that you get in touch with and access as you let go and become more whole and connected to all that you are, which is infinitely greater than the boundaries defined by your skin. In the common analogy, we are just a wave on the ocean, yet always a part of the entire ocean. *Big Mind* is accessed in that consciousness where the wave and the ocean meet. You are still the seemingly separate wave having a meeting with someone or doing whatever you are doing, but you are touching that integrated area where the wave and ocean merge. As the wave, you can express the wisdom of the ocean through you. All you have to do is stop thought and let the wisdom and insight come through. How do you do that? Putting these earlier chapters into practice is a good start.

As a side note: *Big Mind* is not the ultimate end point of meditation, it's just a useful level to reach and have access to while you're learning to live and work in the world. Beyond *Big Mind,* you go beyond breathing to being breathed, and then to becoming the breath and dissolving more and more into the totality. It's like taking a refreshing dip in an endless pool. The next level beyond that is the void, where there really isn't any "there" there, or any "you" to look around and give it a travel rating. You only know you've been there when you come back out – if you ever do.

Four steps into Big Mind:

Step 1: Heal – I am aware that there are shortcuts into the experience of higher consciousness and Big Mind, but all too often, I have watched seemingly successful leaders' work and lives collapse around them when they haven't done the foundational work. Examples litter the political and business arenas as I write this. As they expanded into their power, unresolved childhood issues dislodge from the deeper crevices of their caves and dramatically sabotaged everything they had created. I've seen it cost them their careers, reputations, freedom, their life, and the lives of others. I experienced it personally in another thought leader many years ago. Having power without true consciousness is like a child playing with a loaded gun – someone can get seriously hurt.

Healing your core programming is a prerequisite for quieting the mind, which is essential for all of the other steps. If you have taken the step of healing your emotional backlog, and rewritten your program for getting love, then you have begun to reconnect with those parts of yourself that you once, most likely unknowingly, left behind. These parts are the parts that you were afraid other kids might make fun of or not like, the parts that your dad was uncomfortable with because he hadn't learned to open up to his own issues, the parts that didn't fit Mom's image of who or what you should be, and so on. We learn to hide our scars and fragile areas so that we can feel more accepted and safer in the world. While this may have served us while growing up, it is our raw vulnerability and reclaiming of those cast-off parts of ourselves that make life truly safer and better as an adult. As you continue to use the five steps to look and heal more deeply, opportunities will open up to you along your path. You will be healing and more fully reintegrating that inner child – that whole and complete original perfect being. This is what ultimately creates your unshakable foundation.

"What I recommend for all of us is to come back to ourselves and take care of the little boy or the little girl who inhabits the depth of our wounded soul."
–Thich Nhat Hanh

Step 2: Breathe – Breathing is necessary to go into that emotional backlog deeply enough to fully heal. Your breath is the vehicle that takes you into your cave, into your emotional backlog. That emotion got stuck because you weren't breathing during an earlier event, and so breathing into it is part of how you get that energy unstuck and moving through you and out. Once you've used the breath to heal that old emotional backlog, you are able to effectively rewrite your internal core programming and beliefs to reflect self-acceptance and self-love.

Your breath is like having a built-in mindfulness gauge. By having learned to breathe, you can use your breath as a significant indicator of how on track you are. As I shared with a client the other day, my current gauge is the number of breaths it takes for me to quiet my mind and enter into the silence. Being able to do it in one breath is where I have set my bar.

Your breath is a marvelous gift that you can use to create whatever level of consciousness you wish to live in. It will also fully support you in moving into and through any challenges or rough spots that you run into in life. If you ignore or don't learn how to use this amazing gift, your life is more at the whim of what others want and feel you should be doing. You'll run out of time, pleasing and enabling them so that they feel safe within their comfort zones and are comfortable with and accepting of you. Any enabling causes us to avoid dealing with our own or others' issues. It's a distraction we use so that we don't have to look more deeply or breathe more fully. Yet that's exactly what we need to be doing to address and heal an issue so that we can powerfully express ourselves with an open heart.

Your breath is an exquisitely-designed navigation tool. It can take you anywhere you want to go. Vast untapped territories await, and your breath has you already well-equipped.

Step 3: Integrate – Having breathed into and healed your emotional backlog so that you could rewrite your program for getting love, you have released the negative, unsupportive, subconscious resistance going on in your brain. All these messages told you to play small, play it safe. They had you using the same neurological pathways and not deviating from them. This was your neurological comfort zone. But once you heal that old stuff and release the resistance, you can now use the breath to help you in re-accessing, rewiring, and integrating your whole brain.

The actual brain integration exercises that create new neural pathways are all fun and new physical, mental, and emotional tasks (within realms such as drawing, sound, movement, and language), that allow the different parts of your brain to connect and practice working together. In these processes, people often begin to recognize the innate potentials that they never knew they had. This further supports changes in people's thinking and perception that result in seeing and experiencing ourselves in new and empowering ways. As you open up the chemical gateways and begin to neurologically rewire your whole brain, the different aspects of the brain begin to trust and coordinate their innate abilities. This greater connection, both within your body and within your brain, results in a more focused and quieter mind. It is from this quieter, more present place that we can explore the different degrees of living mindfully.

Step 4: Mindfulness – The breath is your ever-present vehicle that facilitates you in living mindfully enough to continue that forward progression in your life.

As I mentioned earlier, mindfulness is at the heart of every aspect of these steps and of your life. If you aren't living mindfully, then you aren't expanding, and if you aren't expanding, then you're running into resistance and will continue to not have enough time for yourself and your most important work. You know this as well as I do – it's just my turn to help remind you so that you can bring yourself back to a more mindful and conscious place. The extra time you are looking for is right there for you. I promise.

Step 5: Accessing Big Mind – A moment in *Big Mind* can be worth months of trying and efforting in small mind. It's like running a race while only hopping along on one leg. The other leg is there, just as Big Mind is there, just waiting for you to unleash it.

With Big Mind, you more quickly and clearly see what and how you want to take care of a project or aspect of your life. Less time is wasted on false starts and misdirection. You also have a clear plan in your head that leads you through the maze of any aspect of your life. You will be saving time, which leaves you more time for taking care of yourself, your relationships, and for your special projects. You may also just want to hang out more, relax, enjoy. Just a thought.

You know the stories of the major players who have stepped into *Big Mind* and changed the culture with the contributions they brought forth. Jack Canfield shares how he found his *Chicken Soup for the Soul* title in *Big Mind*, Einstein came up with that little thing called the theory of relativity, Picasso rocked the art world with his cubist expressions, and Gandhi changed the politics of the world. How many more examples can you count without even needing to stretch? And you're not limited to just little snatches of insight and wisdom from Big Mind, you can hang-out there and enjoy watching your guidance unfold within you. *Big Mind* is available to you, and you're learning how to access it.

From the powerful place of a quieter mind and a more fully-integrated brain, you can breathe into the stillness and the expansive awareness of *Big Mind* whenever you wish. Of course, the journey really continues into awareness of the true essence of existence, which is the interconnectedness or emptiness. This is the foundation for spiritual awareness – for enlightenment. But that's a different chat.

Big Mind is the most evolved way of working smarter rather than just harder. You know the saying, "Two heads are better than one"? Well, when one head is your quiet and integrated whole brain and the other is Big Mind, this popular quote has never been truer. It's all about letting go of trying and instead, letting Universal Intelligence flow through you. Think of the steps that we have gone over as the combination that unlocks your potential to step up to the next level. You know that we live in an abundant Universe. I'm just saying we can always let go to another level and trust that abundance even more fully.

You know there is always a next level that we can play on. There is always another level of consciousness we can explore and live from. To access *Big Mind* as easily as you breathe, you will need to trust and make that level of trust a way of life. You have, no doubt, experienced accessing the Universal Library before, and I'll bet that it was a pretty great experience. Taking the five steps we're going over here gives you full access. *Big Mind* is always and only a breath away.

In business, creativity used to be relegated to a small department. Now creativity is what composes and drives the top companies. The world is evolving and changing so fast that a person's survival depends on how fully they can embrace change and creatively navigate the opportunities that life presents them. With access to your fully integrated whole brain and to *Big Mind,* you are set. You are the surfer who is in the right place at just the right time to catch that big wave and enjoy the ride of a lifetime.

You can certainly access higher states and *Big Mind* through meditation, but if you want to fully access it within a breath and then enjoy hanging out in it for as long as you'd like, then you will want to have cleared up your emotional backlog and rewritten your program for getting love. By having done the inner healing, your mind is quieter, more adept, and a better receiver. Having healed your core programming also allows you to trust more. This 5 Step process of personal evolution also teaches you how to look within and continually heal as you go and grow through life.

When a challenge comes into your life, you'll know how to breathe and be curious. This allows you to be aware of what you are feeling and needing. You know that if you recognize the root of your challenge as an old childhood issue or some other issue from your past, all you have to do is breathe into and fully acknowledge, express, and release the entangled emotions around that issue. In doing so, you turn that challenge into another healing opportunity and you get to experience even more of who you are. For those who may still be wondering how one goes about discovering and being their "authentic self," this is it!

This five-step process maintains – or even accesses – more of your personal power and keeps your heart open. These two things are really one and the same to me. Our heart energy is incredibly powerful. In fact, I quote a well-known living Master and friend, Chunyi Lin, in saying that, "The brain, or conscious mind, has only 10% of the energy for creating. The heart holds the other 90% of that energy." The more open your heart is, the more powerful you are. From that heightened place, you then continue to access your whole integrated brain, and *Big Mind* is still only a breath away. Time is on your side and you are able to create and use your time doing what you want to be doing.

The famous Tibetan monk, Milarepa, had done some very dark deeds in his younger years. With many more years of maturity, he came to regret his harmful acts and decided to mend his ways. At forty-five years old, he chose exile and went into a cave to meditate, staying there in solitude (except for when some hunters showed up and tried to kill him and take his stuff) for about twenty-two years.

Well into his sixties and a now very evolved being, Milarepa finally returned to his hometown. Being in the midst of familiar people and situations from his past, he was quickly confronted by all of his old emotional stuff. Despite his twenty-two years in the cave and the magnificently high states he attained during his time there as a recluse, those old emotional triggers never got resolved and were, in fact, stickier than he ever realized. Emotionally, it was as if he had never left.

For those who want the incredible connection with *Big Mind* and the extraordinary abilities that are available at that level, they have to have done and must continue to do the inner work. Christ went into the desert for 40 days and 40 nights, dealing with his emotional struggles. Buddha sat under the Bodhi tree, working through his desires, fears, and attachments, all of which ultimately stem from an unresolved emotional backlog. He sat until he worked through it all, and then became enlightened. Keep in mind that this emotional backlog can be around your own life, your family's emotional family tree, or from what Carl Jung called our collective unconsciousness.

Even I went through a spiritual trial of sorts. I was in my early thirties, six years into my devoted study, practice, and service to my spiritual teacher, Rama. One night, following an evening meditation with our spiritual teacher in L.A., my then fiancée came home with me and we settled in for the night as usual. The next morning, she abruptly packed up and told me she was going off to Japan with Rama. I was completely blindsided. One day we had plans of "forever" and the next my beloved fiancée was running off with my guru who had engendered my complete trust and devotion. For three days I was crushed, I was devastated – in complete and utter disbelief. I was crying and literally writhing on the floor in raw, emotional pain.

Yet even throughout that agonizing event, there was a part of me that just watched – celebrated even – trusting that, as I invited and stayed present with the process and any and all emotions that came up, there would be some sort of awakening or transformation on the other side. On my path, I had learned that the more challenging the issue we face, the greater the gifts that ensue. I had never experienced such excruciating emotion before, and just hoped that my painful plunge would somehow be worthwhile.

Three days after a pretty constant meltdown, where I totally stayed present and let myself feel, express, and release all of my emotions around that event, I led my regularly-scheduled Wednesday night meditation at my home. About 25 people came that night. Throughout and even after the meditation, the Light in the room (no, not the plug-in lamp kind of light) was shifting and pulsating, similar to the Northern Lights. My students also witnessed this and were having all kinds of expansive experiences in their meditation. Their reactions varied from stunned to delighted, confused, amazed, and incredulous. Yet they all wanted to know what was going on. What was happening? Where was this all coming from?

While experiences with the Light were not new to me, up until that point I had only ever seen my spiritual teacher exhibit such powers. I had never knowingly been a conduit of such energy before. With the barrage of my student's fantastical shares and questions, I became aware that a new siddha (a spiritual power) had been activated in me.

Over the next few months, several additional new siddhas emerged. I know without a doubt, that the inner work I had done before, coupled with my deep emotional release, is what created the fertile ground for those more expansive powers and energies to flow into and through me. After about six or seven years of using the siddhas in my teachings, I recognized the wisdom of the Zen Buddhists. They understand that siddhas are just another distraction. I have to admit, though, it was fun for a while. Expanding our consciousness and living mindfully is really the only game that counts.

From the powerful place of a quieter mind and a more fully-integrated brain, you can breathe into the stillness and the expansive awareness of *Big Mind*. Of course, the journey really continues into awareness of the true essence of existence, which is embracing the interconnectedness of all of existence. This is the foundation for spiritual awareness – for enlightenment. I hadn't originally planned on talking about this, but it couldn't hurt to just take a little peek.

Chapter 9

Quantum Fields Forever

"The world and its relationships are ... a state of pure infinite potential."
–Lynne McTaggart

It was decades ago, when I was taking a class on quantum physics from Fred Wolf, Ph. D., down in the San Diego area at an alternative university. He had explained to us and presented several research videos that showed how our thoughts actually affect physical reality. Before that time, most researchers were still thinking that things of a non-physical nature like thoughts, expectations, and observation had little, if any, effect on matter. But Dr. Wolf's videos clearly challenged those old beliefs.

I remember Fred bringing into class one day something that looked like homemade observation gadgets. As we peered into them, we got to see how our watching the process changed a wave into a particle when it was being measured or observed. The very act of someone witnessing had a direct effect on the pathway the particle would take. Even after all of the years that have passed, I still find myself understanding and owning that reality on an ever-deeper level. Yes, I know its old hat to many of us now. But really, it's still quite amazing. Why is going to Mars so much more interesting to most people than creating our own World?

> *"One of the fundamental laws of quantum physics says that an event in the subatomic world exists in all possible states until the act of observing or measuring it 'freezes' it, or pins it down, to a single state."*
> –Lynne McTaggart
> The Field: The Quest for the Secret Force of the Universe

If our thoughts can actually have an effect on matter, then why isn't that the next frontier and greatest adventure of our time? It seems that the ancient wisdom of spiritual teachings, as well as quantum physics and neurology, are all leading us toward that same truth – that our thoughts do, indeed, have an effect on matter. Quantum physicists and advanced spiritual teachings also seem to all agree that the further and the deeper you look, the more there is really nothing there.

Back in the early days, I imagine that you may have been taught, as I was, that atoms were the most elemental building blocks of matter. I remember in science class, we were instructed to assemble these rather sturdy-looking Styrofoam models of atoms. We were also informed that the nucleus of the atom, although infinitesimally small, was the solid and stable part. But as it turns out, that's not really accurate either. It turns out these atoms contain little, if anything, we can call solid.

As advancing scientific measuring devices made it possible to look more deeply into matter, researchers discovered an entire sub-atomic level. And the further they looked, the more they discovered that it's all emptiness – there's not really anything there. It is now believed that "quanta" are the true building blocks of all matter. But what are they really made of? How solid are quanta? String theory suggests that there are only string-like shapes of potentialities. They are potentialities in the way that stems cells are before their programming is turned on to become a specific part of an eye or an arm.

So, if the smallest of particles of the building blocks of matter are just potentialities, then what determines which potential they end up manifesting?

Could that determining factor be a Consciousness that is within all of existence and most likely beyond? Is our consciousness part of that bigger Consciousness, and are we really just that Grand Consciousness playing at being "us" in this physical world? Surely, this question has been asked before. But wouldn't you like to find out for yourself who you really are, and what you're actually capable of? What an amazing journey that could be! We might be nothing, and yet, we might be everything. Lions and Tigers and Bears, oh my!

The five steps and everything:

So, you may be wondering how quantum physics ties into the 5 Steps of Personal Evolution. I'm going to connect all the dots, so please be patient with me here. In step one, we're literally going back and revising our core programming, so we can rewrite our program for getting love. In a very real sense, that initial old core program has us looking outside of ourselves for the answers that can only be found within. It is also where our internal noise and busyness comes from. All of our desires, fears, attachments – and our myriad of images and expectations of what people and things should be like – also stem from that old limiting core programming. So, it is safe to say that our old programming is truly the source of our limitations, traumas, and dramas in our life. It's why we are feeling overscheduled rather than being able to open up to and fully embrace the opportunities and gifts that life is offering us.

I'm not suggesting that we should be acting on every opportunity that we see in life. I'm suggesting that, if we are paying attention, we'll be noticing and responding to those that support our highest intention. Why waste time on what doesn't serve us and others for our highest good?

As we rewrite that core programming from one of looking outside of ourselves for love and a sense of who we should be, we are able to start looking within and begin to focus on accepting and loving ourselves. That shift of perspective gives our life a whole new sense of direction. It gives it a higher purpose – to love and accept ourselves completely. While it might seem selfish in the beginning, in truth, it really allows us to bring our uniqueness to the world in a fuller and more authentic way than we could have ever done before. From that grounded, open place, our deepest purpose and passions emerge, allowing us to make our unique contributions and a real difference in the world. Yes, you are most likely already doing that, and I imagine that you may want to take it up a level or two. As you well know, the more deeply you accept and love yourself, the deeper will be your level of connection with all that you are. From that elevated place, rather than adding to the collective fear in the world, you become a force for love, kindness, and acceptance. You model it by who you are and how you are showing up in the world. You are choosing love over fear as your path through life.

Also, in step one, the breathing guides and helps us to go into that cave and to connect with and heal that emotional backlog. Then in steps two through five, we continue to use the breath in life-enhancing ways. The breath and how we breathe is really our direct connection with that consciousness we talked about above. The more we're breathing, the more we're bringing in and being part of that consciousness. Our breathing also helps us in becoming aware of that consciousness. In fact, how we breathe determines our level of consciousness. When I say that, what I'm really saying is: How we breathe determines our awareness of that consciousness, our connection with that consciousness, and our ability to bring that consciousness in and through us to create the best life that we can – the one that is most beneficial for ourselves and others.

In taking those first two steps, we have really already begun the third step, which is the brain integration. Most of us have a very selective brain pattern dominance. Some of us, for example, are more logical (left brain) and self-oriented (reptilian brain), while other are more big-picture or spontaneous (right brain) and socially oriented (mammalian brain). You can watch people's habits – how they dress, how they eat, how they speak. All of these characteristics and personality traits are frequently just the result of a brain dominance that largely is the result of their emotional patterning from their old core programming.

Having rewritten your core programming in step one, your mind becomes quieter. Then, as you begin to more fully use your breath and breathing to become more present and aware, you become more focused and develop an even clearer and higher intention for your life. With this foundation, you are able to begin to shift old brain dominance neurological patterns and more fully use your whole, integrated brain. The two cerebral hemispheres of the brain begin to more fully coordinate and work together as a unified team, accessing new abilities. As they literally begin to work together as a team, you get greater access to the forebrain, "where the stuff of angels is made," according to the director of the National Institute of Mental Health. What he's really saying is, that this is where your imagination, your ability to see the bigger picture, and your connection to that higher consciousness comes in. So, now you not only have a quieter brain, but you also have a brain with heightened abilities, capabilities, and connections.

In step four, we bring in mindfulness. What mindfulness does is to train you to use those new capabilities. You've got your higher intention of loving and accepting yourself. You're also in a higher state of consciousness and breathing into and deepening your connection with the universe with that higher consciousness. Your brain is not having arguments with itself. It's a unified team working in the same direction, with a unified and integrated higher intention. The mindfulness is your practice for that single-pointed focus toward what you want to be, what you want to create, your hero's journey, and your exploration of your capabilities.

The type of mindfulness I teach is of the expanded variety. It brings you into complete focus on your personal growth path and your spiritual journey, which actually, as you know, are really one and the same.

Within these first four steps, you've already changed your life. You've already enhanced your capability as a human being and you're going to be thrilled that you've done that much. But from that expanded place, you begin to recognize that if you get the mind even quieter and you're more present – that is, more capable of being quiet and getting out of the way – then you can access Big Mind. Accessing Big Mind opens you up to a deeper level of connection to this consciousness, to the point where it's flowing right through you as you.

All of the old, limiting filters that you used to have are being removed as you rewrite your core programing, learn to breathe, and connect more fully with consciousness. You're also integrating and using your whole brain, developing your mindfully empowered, single-pointed focus on your highest intention. As a direct result of all of this, you are opened up to Big Mind, which is, as you know by now, really just a part of you. You are directly connected with that Consciousness. You are becoming ever more aware that you are that Consciousness. As you accept and grow into all of this, you begin to let that expanded part of you more fully express through you. While you will still enjoy and benefit from meditation, you no longer have to sit for a half-hour in order to get a snippet from that higher consciousness. It can happen as naturally as sitting on the couch, talking with someone, and being fully in that connected, conscious place, watching as the wisdom comes through. You'll find yourself saying, doing, and suggesting the optimal thing for everyone involved. That's certainly been my experience and that of the others who have done this work.

We can take a look at that next level by continuing our conversation about Quantum Physics, Zen Buddhism, spiritual texts, and ancient texts, since they're really all saying the same thing. They're all describing the unlimited source of potentialities that you can tap into and create your reality from. The five steps I'm introducing you to will have you recognizing, how much is truly available to you in this life experience." Well, when you start understanding the truth about what quantum physics, neurology, and the ancient spiritual texts are saying, (which is the same thing from different perspectives), you realize, "Holy shit – I'm *literally* creating my own reality!" It's no longer a hypothetical kind of new age thing – it's real. Those potentialities are just out there in raw form, and the thing that's going to manifest them – into a form that serves and supports yourself and others – is your focus, your thoughts, and your aligned follow-through. Your intention combined with what you believe and expect to see creates the filters you view the world through and create from. And what you look for, believe, and anticipate dictates what you'll be able to create. First, it's your non-physical energy moving in that direction followed by the physical manifestation of those energies. This is how and why you literally create your own reality.

Fortunately, all of these subtle inner processes I described become refined as you go through your 5 Steps of Personal Evolution process. So, by the time you get to this advanced level, you're coming from a place of, "Wow, I understand how this all works, I know what I want to create, and I choose to pay attention to what I'm thinking and doing." Through this five-step process, you are able to recognize, own, and access your creative ability. You become Master and Commander of your own life, regardless of how it unfolds.

There is a Tibetan meditative practice called Shamatha, which is designed to refine the attention and balance the mind. Followers of this practice have reported that, as their mind gets quieter and quieter, they become aware of their subconscious thoughts. This is the practice by which monks and spiritual seekers expand their consciousness. And so it can be for you, only much faster. With these five steps I've uncovered, developed, and shared over the decades, you too are able to quiet your mind and expand your awareness. So, unlike most people, you won't have those 95% of your subconscious thoughts running your life in ways unbeknownst to you. With attention and practice, those 95% of your previously subconscious thoughts become part of your conscious awareness.

Another benefit of these five steps is that, as you are working with and healing those once-subconscious thoughts, you're making sure they are in alignment with your conscious thoughts (the 5%). Those conscious thoughts now include, "I choose to love and accept myself." This makes for a very strong and non-distracting foundation from which your other empowering and supportive thoughts, beliefs, and actions will now arise. Those 95% of your thoughts, which may have had a whole different agenda, are now in complete alignment with that 5%. So, now you've got 100% of who and what you are heading in the same direction. You're like a rocket with enough propulsion to move you through and out of the resistance, and up into the space of the pure potential you get to choose and create from.

As we live from that level of expanded awareness and functioning, we get to consciously create, or at least fully participate in, all aspects of our life. We're writing our own script and the Universe has our back. (Actually, it has our everything, but you know what I mean.) This quantum shift in who we recognize ourselves to be – and this more adept way we are able to function – really causes us to pause and re-define what it means to be human, because we have skyrocketed our capabilities up to a whole new level.

For an influential leader such as yourself, think about the impact you can make when you're harnessing that level of ability, attention, and creative genius. As a transformational leader who is choosing to live on that leading edge, you fully recognize the incredible potential of those you serve. You see them for who they truly are and want to do whatever you can to help them wake up to and harness their incredible potential. You know that this is how they, too, will upgrade their whole life and enrich the lives of all those they serve. You hold that space for them. You supportively guide and encourage them. You do this better than anyone because of the work you have done on yourself – because of who you are being.

You have upgraded and redefined what you want to do and how you want to do it. If you want to continue to lead the parade, this is the leading edge. As you own and use these amazing capabilities, you help and support your community members to expand into their higher level of functioning as well. In this higher level of being, it's important for you, as a leader, to focus beyond treating symptoms, offering shortcuts, and sharing quick fixes. You get to step up and play fully in this opportunity of creating a unified consciousness within each person. And this, in turn, helps create the higher collective unified consciousness that results in a better world for everyone.

String theory?

Advance disclaimer: I hesitated to include this story, because I know that for some readers, it might sound pretty fantastical. I am just candidly relaying my experience here. But I do want you to know that there were absolutely no mind-altering (or any other) substances involved in my desert experience, or at all during this spiritual exploration period of my life.

My purpose in sharing this story is to introduce you to an even deeper level of letting go and the understandings that you may take away from it. Yes, it still is solving your time challenges as it gives you an entirely new perspective of time and space that supports your continued journey into living a fully connected and integrated life with all that you truly are. With this greater perspective, you have fewer attachments to the small stuff and come to a fuller awareness that "it's all small stuff."

In my late twenties, I spent half a dozen years or so with a spiritual teacher who was quite powerful and would often take us out in the desert where we'd explore alternate realities and states of consciousness. We'd often stay out quite late into the night when the energies of the world were quiet. One particularly clear desert night stands out for me. We had moved to several different locations to meditate, each with a different feel and sense of energy. As we settled in at the last one, I sat up straight, breathed fully, and began to quiet my mind. It seemed as if I'd just started when I began to feel myself being drawn out of my body. As

I continued to breathe and let go, I was aware of my body being left behind like a discarded tin can on the desert floor.

As I continued to breathe and merge into the expanse around me, I began to feel like I was being breathed by the universe. I continued to let go and could sense my "self" becoming that breath. Like water spilled on a carpet, I was merging into and becoming one with the fabric of existence. As the space between the threads of existence became much greater, I felt how I was becoming that breath. And as the spaces became still greater, I had the experience of falling through a field of golden luminous threads or strings. Expanding even beyond that, there was no more "me" to see or to witness, as I completely dissolved into the infinite.

As I began to reemerge with a subtle awareness of self, I found myself being drawn back down towards the earth, towards the desert, towards that discarded body that had once been me. I found myself sliding back into that carcass. It all felt strangely familiar, but I would never be the same. However much of what we call "time" went by, there is no way to tell. But from that experience, I still wonder if those luminous golden strands I witnessed were what I would later hear being referred to as the strings in the string theory of quantum physics. Was I, as a dash of consciousness, sprinkled into the stew of creation and given the gift of "seeing" the unlimited potentiality of existence? Perhaps I'll never know, but I do know that in the years and decades that followed, the further I would go within the silence or the light, the less there was of me and that solid existence that we refer to as the here and now. Each time I let go and dissolved completely into what I'd call existence, and then into the void, less was always more, but the more was always emptiness.

I recently read a great book called *Stilling the Mind* by B. Alan Wallace where he is interpreting Shamatha teachings from the Tibetan monk, Dudjom Lingpa. He talks about how relaxing and stabilizing the mind results in your ability to detect increasingly subtle mental processes that may linger for seconds. He shares that, "Mental states and processes that were previously unconscious are now illuminated with the clear light of consciousness. This truly becomes a path of knowing yourself in the sense of plumbing the depths of your own mind."

While this is certainly in alignment with the 5 Steps of Personal Evolution that I offer, where your mind grows quieter and more focused, Lingpa also shares some deeper guidance that is incredibly wise. In the process he describes, Lingpa recommends that we, "Don't grasp ... it (thoughts or images)... Be like a tourist traveling from the surface of your mind, all the way down into its depths. Don't become a homesteader until you reach your destination – the substrate consciousness (the ground of becoming)."

As we talked about earlier, there is always another level to play on. And this level is when, "All appearances and mental states dissolve into ultimate reality ... in other words, they dissolved into the emptiness." In his teachings, Alan Wallace talks about how, "The realization of emptiness prepares the way to recognize your own face, your own nature, your dharmakaya (or Buddha) mind." In these ancient teachings, they are saying that the whole of samsara (existence) and nirvana (enlightenment, heaven) "is not grounded in anything inherently existing." As Wallace shares, even in the Christian faith, "The Gospel of John states that, 'In the beginning was the Word.'" And it was with and from that Word, that mankind came into existence.

Perhaps the flood of hints that we have gotten from our spiritual and scientific realizations are telling us a truth that can only be fully understood by letting go of old beliefs and limitations, by quieting and exploring our mind, and by accessing and playing on an entirely new level. Perhaps we're in the middle of an amazing stage of evolution that you may want to be part of. With all of the evidence that we are much, much more than what we are experiencing, even beyond your current successes, there are so many new levels to explore and enjoy.

As you well know and may even teach, we need to remain focused on what it is we want, staying present and taking action on the daily action steps as they come along. These 5 Steps of Personal Evolution are critical to your continued expansion. The little wiggles and niggles of life are just the gifts that wake us up to the opportunities that are available to us in our life. As I mentioned before, taking these steps will likely, in the beginning, require some courage and repetition. But as you continue to use and apply the processes in these steps, they become second nature and will serve you immensely in fully benefiting from all that life offers you.

Success is relative to the goals we look forward to achieving. We don't want to be like the musician who spends their entire life singing the same songs they wrote and performed decades before. As an influential leader, we want to explore and discover the next gateway that we can open to our tribe. We want to continually advance our evolution and understanding, hone our skills, better our results. We choose to walk the path of a true master: ever-new, ever-curious, ever-discovering. We want our "next" to draw out the very best of who and what we are. Regardless of our age or our current level of success, we are still on the journey. Being grateful and present with that journey allows us to find our way, all the way Home.

Chapter 10

The Slippery Slope

"If you do not change direction, you may end up where you are heading."
—Lao Tzu

The question beginners on the personal or spiritual path (they're really the same) used to ask is, "How will I know when I'm done?" The answer, "When you're not here anymore," was always delivered with a smile.

Regardless of what age we consciously begin our inner journey, our mind will be like that of a young child walking from one end of a carnival to the other. In the beginning, every bell or barker's call grabs our attention. I remember just after my very first meditation, thinking that the process had made my mind noisier rather than quieter. It didn't take long before I realized that, no, what was actually happening was that I was becoming aware of just how noisy my mind already was.

The five steps we've been chatting about are all part of the process of quieting the mind, so that, over time, you can walk from one end of that carnival to the other without losing focus on the light at the other end. The carnival noise is, of course, all of the desires, fears, images, and attachments that we've developed around who and what we need to be to survive, to be accepted, and to be loved. Having spent our formative years, and likely even decades, looking outside of ourselves to handle all of our desires, fears, images, and attachments, we have become conditioned to keep looking outside.

All of this inner noise and outer distraction keeps us from being able to quiet and use our whole, integrated brain. That means we're using a great deal more time and energy to accomplish the work we are doing in our life. False starts, dead ends, re-dos, and uncertainties take up much of the time that we could be otherwise using to take care of ourselves, our relationships, and to dive in to the projects that beckon us. By resolving the source of that noise, and being able to quiet and focus the mind, we can optimize our time and how we use it. We can revel in having more than enough time to take care of ourselves and enjoy our life.

I'm not sure, but it appears that for many people, the idea of looking within is either totally foreign or clearly something they would never ever want to do. On a recent visit to the dentist to have my teeth cleaned, the new hygienist asked me what I did for work. I briefly explained how I guided people into the deepest sources of their issues and the greatest possibilities for their life. She looked at me incredulously and, as if she were tasting something very nasty, said, "Why would anybody ever want to do that?" Fear over love, or love over fear. That is always our choice.

Challenges along the way:

While it's great that you are playing on the CEO level, you have probably become aware that personal challenges and growth opportunities are a bit more subtle and harder to see from that refined place where you have already fine-tuned much of your life. Of course, partners, your kids, and life will always seem quite happy to point out areas where you still need to do some work! In playing on these higher levels, I know that you have done a lot of work and have a whole quiver of tools at the ready. The challenge is that identifying the deeper issues by ourselves, and determining how to best handle them, often becomes more and more subtle and difficult to notice. "You can't see the forest for the trees," as the old saying goes. This is exactly the place where working with a knowledgeable and experienced guide who has a bigger (and unattached) perspective becomes invaluable. This is the point where Tiger Woods would get a putting coach. That outside perspective is essential to both see and help integrate the subtle shifts that the master needs to make.

Since it is the ongoing change of our existence that facilitates our own personal transformation, it seems like it would be easy for us to just roll along with that change like a raft on the river, "Row, row, row your boat, gently down the stream..." and all that. The challenge that I've run into, and I'm presuming is somewhat the same for you, is that you're not the only one in the boat. There are life partners, business partners, kids, and cats, and the boatload of people who are relying on and trusting you to help them chart their course and handle both the rough seas and calm waters ahead.

While you might be in trust of the universe, and in a "let's go, hi-de-ho!" mode, others in your tribe might be in more of a "hell no, I won't go" place. Frequently they're coming from an "I want you and our life to be just the way it is." mode. Any changes you make may rock the boat and reveal the inherent discomforts of the comfort zone. You may unconsciously, and over time even consciously, feel that if you take your life up to the next level, it may cost you your primary relationship, or maybe your tribe won't follow, or, or, or ... I get it; it's scary stuff.

Wouldn't it be so much easier to just be and do what they all want and expect of you? It seems a lot easier to just not talk about those taboo topics that may make someone uncomfortable. Why make the effort to go deeper within and heal, and to reintegrate a precious part of who and what you are, when your tribe may not welcome that new part of you with open arms? Why rock the boat when everything is going along so well? One reason is that change is happening anyway, and if you don't go with the flow, you'll eventually get beached on a sandbar!

Another reason is that it's your job; it's part of your role as leader of the tribe. You're the captain and it's your job to set the course when the winds of change are blowing. Would you have wanted to stay stuck where you were five or ten years ago? Do you want to look back from five or ten years in the future and see that you got stuck where you are now? That's not who you are. That's not how your life works. The song isn't "Sit, sit, sit in your boat, keep the anchor down." It's "Row, row, row the darn thing, and stay conscious and aware enough to enjoy the ride!"

I'm sorry, I really am, but if we can't laugh at ourselves, then what's the point? Perhaps you're feeling older and a bit tired. Maybe you've reached and surpassed those amazing goals you set for yourself many years ago, and it feels like it's time to just glide along for a while. Maybe you're even kidding yourself that if you just get this next project done, then you'll be done. I get it – golfing, boating, no expectations or demands, it does have its allure. The only problem is that you'll be sitting in that perfect spot, looking out at that perfect view, having that perfect drink, and you'll notice your mind exploring that special project or book that you never got done. You know the one I'm talking about: that pinnacle project or goal that was so exceptional, it would have required you to take your consciousness and your life up to the next level in order to successfully achieve it. Could that be why your soul persists in calling you toward it?

"When do you know when you're done?" For those who are on their path, and care and want to support and serve others on their path, it's when you're not here anymore. Though, over time, things will change and will certainly look different, breath-by-breath and step-by-step, you will still be called to explore around the next corner and over the next hill of your life. Maybe you feel that the "you" that you are, isn't up for it. Maybe you feel that you, in your present state, can't or just don't want to take it further. I'd suggest that you're probably right, and that it is time for you to upgrade your brain, your energy, and your life to prepare yourself for the next leg of your journey. Will your entire tribe follow? Perhaps, and perhaps not. But the ones who are truly on the adventure with you will giggle and wiggle and, after taking a few deep breaths, look to you to show them the way. Your job is to open the doorways and invite the others through. Hi-de-ho!

As you well know, even the most successful, advanced, and conscious beings amongst us still have their blind spots. While we all have a literal scotoma, or blind spot, on the head of our optic nerve, we also have figurative blind spots in how we see ourselves and the world. We often just can't see things that another may see quite clearly. I know my wife is happy to point out my blind spots for me on a regular basis, whether I want to hear about them or not. A few of my closest friends and I also have a deep enough connection that pointing out what the other may have missed is a normal and welcome part of our conversations. Without the outside perspective of others, we'd remain partially blind and unaware. Without those outside perspectives and support, we may find ourselves unnecessarily running up against repetitive and unsupportive patterns and limitations. We don't see how certain elusive thoughts, beliefs, or patterns of ours may be causing us to not use our time as well as we could, or to falter in taking care of ourselves and certain areas of our life that we value.

Tiger has his swing coach, and the greats in tennis, business, politics, or any field have their coaches for just this very reason. Yes, I know I'm dating myself by referring to Tiger, but I do love watching him play. His level of presence and focus back in the day was incredible to watch. And who knows, if he had taken these steps, he might still be in the game.

I've had a lot of clients throughout my life who came in having already done a lot of great, deep, emotional work. They meditate, they're mindful, and they've really cultivated success in their life. But still they found themselves challenged and not playing as fully as they'd like in certain areas of their life. Perhaps they're not taking care of themselves physically as well as they'd like, or they're having challenges in their significant relationship, or with their kids, or they want to take their work up to the next level, but they're feeling stuck where they are. In each and every case in our work together, we've always found the parts where they were stuck. These turned out to be either their personal blind spots, or some other insidious little part that just hadn't been fully dealt with.

It could be a particular emotion like anger, hurt, fear, or shame that they didn't fully acknowledge, express, and release. Maybe they didn't get back to a level of understanding, appreciation, forgiveness, and love. Even though they have done some great work around their parents and family, there's now another layer they're ready to take a look at and resolve. Since our significant relationship is really a reflection of our relationship within ourselves, often times our personal work helps establish that deeper connection within, and that deeper inner connection is then, of course, reflected in our most significant relationship, and all our other relationships. One thing we can count on is that the gifts in life continue to come. Whether we recognize, receive, and open them is up to us. Regardless of how much we've done and grown, there's always an opportunity to deepen our connection within and to expand our consciousness and awareness.

You probably see a lot of people out there doing a lot of great work, but still falling short of the level of results they want. The degree that they are falling short is often parallel to the degree that they haven't done their inner work. Yes, there is always another level and there always will be. But it is those areas of our life that we are not able to see that create the resistance and limitations in our life. It makes no difference whether those blind spots are from the past or the present; they limit our life just the same. It's like the flow of electricity or water; the smaller the wire or the pipe, the greater the resistance there will be, and the more the flow becomes constricted. In other words, it doesn't matter how much energy and information is available to you at the source, only how much can get through to be used and expressed as you wish in your life.

The more you enlarge the wire or expand the size of the pipe via continuing to use these five steps, the greater the flow of energy and information will be to and through you. That greater flow results in your having the time and ability to more easily create and manifest what you dream of. I know that you know this, yet it's fun to remember this together.

Please keep in mind that the first few times you use these five steps, they will take some time and conscious attention, but as you integrate the practice more and more fully into your life, they become relatively automatic. A circumstance that might have once resulted in your momentarily catching or even holding your breath, will later be an event or circumstance that triggers you to remember to consciously breathe and move right through a challenge – no getting stuck. With practice, it will all be so automatic, that you won't even notice that there's anything going on that would have, at one time, been confronting or challenging for you.

I remember how overwhelmed I felt when I started taking a friend's black-belt-level tae kwon do class. One of the challenges was that I wasn't a black belt. While much of what we were doing was just a modification of a known and well-practiced move for the rest of the class, for me it was all brand new. I was also at least twice the age, if not a lot more, than most of the other students.

Okay, I'll quit whining now. But my point is that within a few months, I knew several of the forms well enough that I was having a great time. The amazing plasticity of my brain was at work, firing and rewiring new levels of proprioception, balance, and enhanced awareness of my movement in space and time. While it would take years before I could master the art, I found how it was naturally being woven into my life.

After a lovely dinner outside on a deck with my son and his wife, I got up and took a step back. The only problem was, there was no deck there! While I faltered for a moment as I found my balance, I did not fall down. I completely credit the tae kwon do practice I'd done for my relatively graceful recovery. The point is, that it's not just one area of your life that changes, but even the day-to-day little things that positively upgrade and shift when we are clear, aware, integrated, and playing on a higher level. A good recovery is better than falling on our butt any day.

Doing this work yourself does not mean that you necessarily have to integrate it into the work you do with others. It just means that with your having gone deeper and coming from a clearer, more supportive and empowered place, you are able to go deeper in your relationships – both with the people who work with you and those who learn from you. I've had a lot of therapists come to work with me over the years, because they realized that they couldn't take their clients into areas or depths that they hadn't journeyed into and become comfortable with within themselves. It's not like they had to change how they did their work; they were just bringing an enhanced version of themselves to it, which benefitted everyone.

It is difficult to watch people, who seem to truly want to change their life, run into the same challenges again and again. They do much of the outer work, and experience times where they feel like they are finally moving in the right direction. They take this or that course that focuses on one or another of the symptoms of unresolved deeper issues. Don't get me wrong, there is certainly value in various works, like trying to find out how to better manage your time, market your business, lose weight, hone your purpose, passion, authentic expression, etc. etc. Yet without doing the deeper inner work, these processes really end up just being quick fixes for relieving the symptoms that crop up from a lack of inner healing, alignment, and integration.

Like much of what we see in our medical model, we get rid of the symptoms of a problem with this or that pill, but never really look at or deal with the underlying lifestyle causes of the problem. The more our healthcare system fails us, the more pills that are created to get rid of the ever-escalating, obvious symptoms. While we might lose weight with a diet or by taking a pill, the underlying emotional stress that's causing us to overeat just surfaces in other ways through different symptoms. Symptom chasing has become a multi-billion-dollar industry. It's so profitable precisely because it doesn't work – not because it does.

We can take care of all of the more evident symptoms that we want, but, unless we go in and discover the deeper root cause of a challenge, we will still be living with the problem. As a chiropractor, I saw this all the time. "Doc, if you could just adjust my neck, or help me with this low back pain...." Week after week, month after month, they'd come back and tell me how great a job I'd done, and then ask, "Just please, do it again." Meanwhile, when I asked them about how they were doing with the lifestyle changes I'd recommended and were needed to truly fix the source of their problem, they'd shyly turn the conversation in some other, more comfortable direction.

A little truth that I learned while doing some research in Chiropractic school is that approximately eight out of the ten of the most common reasons that people die are the direct result of lifestyle choices. I remember thinking to myself, "Wow, so what a lot of people are doing is just consciously or unconsciously choosing how they want to commit suicide." They worry about not having enough time for this or that, but then end up cutting ten or more years off their life, or profoundly diminishing the quality of their life by not being present enough to take good care of themselves. Yes, it takes some time to go through this 5 Step Personal Evolution process. But the tradeoff is, if you take the time to go through this process, then you will absolutely have the time and ability to do whatever it is that you truly want to do. It's that same principle of sharpening the saw before cutting down the tree. If you want to save time and get the job done faster and more efficiently, you've got to first sharpen your leading edge.

Personally, I'm not too attached to how long I live, but I certainly want to be living as full and fulfilling a life as I can during my time here. I want to explore who I am, who we truly are, and all the amazing things that we are capable of doing and being. So far, my journey has been absolutely mind-blowing. Comfortable or not, no part of it has ever let me down.

The subtleness of sabotage:

Imagine it's getting late, and you're enjoying reading a good story. Your eyes begin to get tired and slowly close. What seems like only a moment later, you come to again, but perhaps the screen on your Kindle has gone off, or the book has slid down onto your chest. You perhaps go through this same process a few more times before calling it a night and going to sleep. Well, that's pretty much how many people unconsciously let themselves fall asleep in their life.

Over time, we get used to not having as much energy as we hoped to have. We unconsciously don't breathe as regularly or as fully as we know would be healthier for us. We settle into a life that reflects our current mental abilities and level of awareness, usually paying attention only to what we have to, when we have to.

Well, that's really how subtly the unresolved issues, limitations, and challenges from our past can distract us from playing on the level that we'd truly like to be playing on. It can be the littlest things that people say to us, or how they treat us, that can weave their way into our sense of who and what we are. I remember one day when I was sixteen. I had just heard about something called meditation and had a cool colored light in my room that I focused on. This was probably 1963 and very off-the-wall stuff. Anyway, I was watching this light and unknowingly quieting my mind as I focused my attention. From out of nowhere, I was struck with the crystal-clear awareness that I wanted to be a writer. It was my first grand "aha!"

I jumped up and ran into the kitchen and excitedly told my dad about my vision and new-found direction. Within seconds, and all with the best of intentions, he calmly explained that being a writer would never make any money, and that I should really shoot for a position as a foreman for the Gas Company – then I'd be set. I was, of course, disappointed, and moped back into my room. His intentions were certainly good, and it seems like such an innocent little exchange between a son and a father who cares about him. But what really happened was he'd pulled the rug right out from under me. That one little comment extinguished my dreams and took a whack at my self-image as well. Later, as an adult on my path, it literally took years to extract those threads of doubt and limitation that my dad had unknowingly woven into the tapestry of me. In truth, it took decades.

How many of those little moments – with parents, siblings, friends, school teachers, bosses, coaches, clergy, and others – are stored in our neurological memory and the emotional backlog in our gut? How many of these impactful moments have we forgotten or hardly noticed at the time? Yet all of these little experiences have colored who we've become. While the deeper work I referred to in chapter three resolves the core issues and programming, these subtler threads tend to fray and stick out in various ways in our life. Each of these random threads subtly contributes to the resistance within us, preventing us from playing as fully as we are capable. Each draw on our energy flow, acts as energy leaks, and subtly contracts our definition of "self." Those old disempowering patterns and thoughts, over time, become part of our identity, expressed as personality traits that we excuse and even defend.

You have, no doubt, done a lot of great work to get to the level of success that you enjoy – yet as we expand, we open up new layers of those subtler issues. We then need to mindfully breathe into and supportively deal with and heal them. As we do, those subtle issues stop sabotaging and start empowering us. As you learn to be mindful and present during and with your life, you will be able to notice these subtler threads and carefully reweave them into a more supportive pattern. Each time you do this, you are remembering and accepting more of who you truly are. You are becoming a more whole and integrated being. As you continue using this work to heal and evolve, your unique purpose, passion, expression, and authenticity shine ever more brightly. You use your focused energy and clarity to serve and support others, as is your mission. Your big contribution, from this place of higher awareness, higher vibration, and expanded abilities, lights the way for all of us to be able to see and appreciate the tapestry and potential of our human culture.

Our healing is not a "one and done" kind of thing. Often, when I overhear people talk about personal growth, I'll hear someone authoritatively tell their friends about some workshop that they took decades before. Their "been there done that" attitude implies that the one weekend was all that anyone would ever need to have fully taken care of the past and to be able to live the rest of their life free of unresolved issues. Boy, I sure wish that were the case! But having had the privilege of guiding thousands of people – many of whom have already done some great work – I know that just is not how it works. That's like someone saying they did all the gardening ten years ago; why would they ever have to do it again? In the same way, this cultivation of you in your personal evolution is a lifetime journey.

Mark's story:

I met Mark many years ago when we were both part of a spiritual community. We'd run into each other from time to time. He was always a very bright guy, a good businessman, and a lovely person with a kind and gentle heart. He knew my background and that I'd continued with meditations and personal growth work long after we'd left that group, so when we'd see each other, he'd often comment how he was going to quit drinking for a while and start doing yoga and eating better. I'd always respond how that was a great idea, and I'd wish him well. In between the times when I'd see him, he'd be back to partying and over-drinking and eating. As several decades passed, this pattern continued.

He was always about to – or had just made some effort to – get himself back on track. I knew that he had had a difficult childhood, with alcoholic parents who both died when he was in his late teens, so I understood what he was dealing with. He always seemed quite interested in what I was doing, but would become quite defensive if I made the slightest suggestion about how he might use some of the work to help with his identified challenges. After a few growls, I got the message and kept my thoughts to myself.

Mark would be a good example of a person who had taken the weekend workshop and dabbled in this and that, but never done the deeper work. By the way, Mark really does have all the potential in the world. His resistance is not uncommon, just unfortunate, since it is the very thing that is holding him back from the healthy, loving, and fulfilling life he really desires and is worthy of.

Even when he'd put in a serious effort at changing his life, Mark would fall back to his old, established, unsupportive patterns. I have to admit, it was hard in some ways for me to witness his struggle and repeated efforts over the decades. He'd keep trying to make the shifts he said he wanted, only to then slip back again and again.

It's kind of like having an overweight friend who works really hard to lose a bunch of weight, and then ends up just gaining it back, many times over. It looks difficult. They're following all the "just do this or that" quick fixes, but over the long run, these strategies just aren't working. It's tough to watch as these loved ones sometimes begin to feel that they must be flawed in some way. Instead of feeling better about themself, they can start to lose confidence, and just want to give up. I get it: Seeing results gives us hope, while sliding down that slippery slope of trying and efforting, only to then slide back down to what feels like square one, is no fun at all.

I get the value and attraction of the quick fix information, but without the deeper work, it's generally not enough to bring about the lasting change or improvement that we're looking for. Instead of helping, it can actually end up just being another red mark on an already too long list of perceived failures. That backlog of unacknowledged and unexpressed emotions invisibly sabotages us like black ice on the hill of success. I've personally experienced it, and I imagine that you may have also.

These aren't just my five steps, they are the five inner steps, insights, tools, and practices that I have directly seen work in my own life and in the lives of thousands of clients. They are a culmination of ancient and proven spiritual guidance together with leading edge science, culled into practical, actionable steps for living a happy, successful, and fulfilling life. These are the steps that result in true and lasting transformation. With over forty-five years of paying very close attention, I have watched countless times how when someone tries to avoid one of these steps, they either end up playing smaller than they'd envisioned, or saying to heck with the whole idea of changing their life at all. As a transformational leader, I know that you want to help people and support them on their journey. As you more consciously use these five steps, you will take yourself and your work up to a whole new level. From that place, everyone wins.

It does take a certain level of humility and a willingness to be vulnerable in order to remain mindful enough to notice the subtle cues and gifts that life offers us. Yet it is in this open and curious state of mind – the beginner's mind, as the Zen folks talk about – that you will find and comfortably enjoy living on the leading edge of your chosen and fulfilling life. You'll find that you consistently practice an openness to ongoing healing, subtly using your breath to mindfully access your brain's innate abilities, and allowing yourself to be guided at will, through your connection with *Big Mind*. In this conscious way of living, you can relax and settle your life down as much as you want. The role I've chosen (or perhaps been assigned) is that of a coach or a guide, supporting you in opening up more fully to your Self.

It's like the successful "you" that you are, can't fulfill your next expanded dream until you go within and breathe life into the expanded "you" that can. In order to have enough time to take better care of yourself, your relationship, and create that special project or write that life-transforming book, you will want to access more of your Self from those unexplored depths within. Those parts are there; they want to play; they're just waiting to be invited to the party. Then of course, the process of creating that next project will give them the opportunity to integrate and create together, which also results in your further evolving. Yes, it's a set-up. And a really fun one at that. In this amazing game, the player always wins!

I had the opportunity to interview Dr. Rudy Tanzi a couple of times. Along with being a great guy, he is a Harvard Professor who is a pioneer in Alzheimer's research. Talk about using the whole brain – Rudy's range of talents is quite diverse. He is an expert in the accumulation of beta amyloids in the brain, and he has also jammed with Aerosmith. You might know him as the co-author with Deepak Chopra of the books like, *Super Brain*, where they wrote about unleashing the power of your brain, and their latest book *The Healing Self.* Dr. Tanzi estimates that by the year 2030, over 50% of people over 65 years old will have lost their mind to Alzheimer's, and only 5% of those cases are due to genetic predisposition. That means the other 95% are due to lifestyle choices. In other words, we are in a very real, "use it or lose it" situation.

I watched my mom in her later years completely forget who she was, as well as everyone she'd ever known, including me. She'd ramble on about fictionalized stories of her life that changed from day to day, making it clear for me that valuing and making the rest of my life worthwhile was really the only choice to make. I totally get wanting to just settle down, but the hidden cost of those seductive comfort zones is a death of sorts that I don't wish to choose. Expanding my consciousness beyond any physical expression of self and integrating into the oneness while meditating in the garden is an image that works better for me.

We are either expanding or contracting, becoming more or less aware. Yes, many people enjoy staying in a fixed range of fluctuation, expanding out a little and then contracting back in a little – staying in their idealized comfort zone. While fear, doubt and resistance are a normal part of dealing with change, "Normal can never be extraordinary." (William Martin) The real art of life is to explore the fullness of who and what we are. The game of discovering what you are all about and are really capable of, will continue to make your life so worthwhile. Yes, I know I'm preaching to the choir, but I'm just reminding myself and the rest of the choir to keep on singing the song of life.

In all honesty, there are ways that we can take this journey on our own. Sometimes, in very extreme situations (think Viktor Frankl – *Man's Search for Meaning*), we're left with little choice – either expand or die. While it takes a village to raise a child, it also takes a Sanga (spiritual community) to raise a consciousness. And, while we absolutely can expand and heal on our own, it is so much easier when assisted by a guide who knows this path and can help you on your inner journey. Without a guide, those blind spots we talked about often sneak in and sabotage your ability to stay focused on breathing through those dark or unconscious places, short-changing your ability to mindfully access your full potential.

If we just keep breathing throughout, then life unfolds quite perfectly. But after years of watching, I can assure you that when we're in the process of shifting our life to the next level, we often don't have the perspective we need to see those blind spots. Most people don't even realize how often they aren't really breathing, which is the gas pedal of the change we're looking for. And since every journey is as unique as the person who takes it, it is also quite tricky to be asking yourself the right questions to take yourself down into those inner knowings that you don't yet know that you know. And, wherever you do hit a little snag or bump up against your own resistance, how easy will it be to guide yourself through that resistance? Just as you wouldn't perform your own dental work (unless you're Tom Hanks stranded on some remote island), my experience has shown me that seeking the guidance of a skilled professional will always get you far superior results.

With the perspectives and support of a guide who is intimately familiar with the terrain of our inner worlds, what may otherwise take decades for you trying to navigate on your own can happen within months. In my work with clients, mostly influential leaders, the ones who have made the biggest impact are those who are ready to choose love over fear. The outcome of this work really boils down to that: being and practicing love over fear as a way of life. Oh, the places you'll go!

And then there's my own mission; I too, am in the legacy chapter of my life. At my age, the best way for me to positively influence millions of people around the world is to make sure that the influential leaders I work with have all of the support, guidance, and integration that they need. I work with the best so that they can be at their best. This is my wish for you. Breathe and heal; breathe and take that next step on your journey. It will make a world of difference in your life and everyone else's.

Change remains the one constant in our life. I understand that it's scary, but I also understand, as I imagine you do, that if we don't make these changes within ourselves, they won't be reflected within our society. The systems that our society relies on will continue to fail. We will continue to have conflict and greater disconnection between ourselves. And we will continue to destroy our ability to live harmoniously, supportively, and sustainably in this lovely planet we call home. We're either learning to love more fully, or we are letting fear control our life. As a inspirational leader, your life and your choices are critical to the direction society moves in. For the sake of our children, for the sake of our children's children, I trust that you will continue to make the choice to expand into the Love that you are.

Conclusion

Moving into the End Zone

*"There are only two mistakes one can make along the road to truth:
not going all the way, and not starting."*
–Buddha

L ife is a marvelous journey filled with wonderful adventures. As we go through our life there is the one thing that we can count on, and that is change. Each year we get a little older and, as we mature, we also expand our life experience. Our sense of self and who we are continues to grow. At first our house and yard are the world we know, then we discover the neighborhood, and the woods across the street. There is always more out there to discover as our world expands.

As much as we thrive on the adventures in life, coming home when we are tired is always a welcome part of the journey. Coming home to what we know and trust, our own bed, our family, our life, is really coming home to our comfort zone. The thing we notice, though, is that each time we return from our hero's journey, we are a little different. Our perspective has shifted. Where we once saw challenge, we now recognize opportunity. We're embracing life with our heart more open.

If you're at all like me, then with each of your hero's journeys, you have probably first initially struggled or resisted – fighting with your demons and dragons, only to later find out that they were actually allies, and, in truth, a core part of yourself that you are rediscovering. And as you discover and reintegrate those disparate parts of yourself, you find yourself returning home, feeling and being more whole and renewed. Each adventure is another stage of your personal evolution, where you are becoming more and more your whole and authentic self again. That "changed home" you return to is your new and upgraded comfort zone. Each new comfort zone you enter reflects your heightened and expanded level of being, where you breathe, enjoy, relax, and unleash your creativity. In time, you will again be called to your next hero's journey. This is an ongoing process – one that makes your life extraordinary.

In having rewritten your core programming for life, you'll find that you're less at the effect of the past and any subconscious sabotage. You'll find yourself being able to breathe more fully and deeply. You'll be more present and aware. In that mindful state, you'll be able to access enhanced whole-brain thinking, imagination, and creativity. Functioning as a more whole, integrated being, you will develop an even higher intention in life as greater access *to Big Mind* guides you in fulfilling your most meaningful dreams.

How do you know when it's time for your next hero's journey? Well, you now know that those issues or challenges in your life are indicators that you're being called to the next level. You've already been moving toward that expansion, whether consciously or unconsciously. You'll know when it's time to shift again because you'll start noticing the "niggles." Your current comfort zone will start to feel uncomfortable. Even if you at first resist, you'll soon remember that your hero's journeys are the best part of life. You are an evolving, expanding, remarkable being who welcomes your evolution however it arises.

Enjoy the Journey, my friend. It is truly the adventure of a lifetime.

Acknowledgments

I have been blessed. My life has been an incredible adventure - a fine blend of the mystical, the magical, and the opportunity of living and loving in the world. The worst parts of my life have become the greatest gifts. My teachers have been my parents, friends, students, clients, and so many others whose lives have shown me the infinite possibilities and choices we all have.

I have worked with and learned from some of the very best. I have also learned from the struggles and pain of those feeling broken in their most desperate hours. Nature taught me how life could look at its finest, my own inner struggles showed me how life could look at its worst. Throughout it all, the Breath has been my teacher, guide, and trusted companion. It helped me to heal and remember, and to merge with the infinite. My lovely wife Carol taught me how to love. I was, no doubt, and perhaps still am, a challenging student.

From very early on in my life, I've had a very intimate relationship with the consciousness that expresses and is expressed by all of existence and beyond. Letting go and merging with that consciousness is the easy part for me. It is a delight I deeply embrace. The "living and working in the world" part has been a bit more of a challenge. And I think, perhaps, that I'm beginning to get the hang of it.

My joy is in supporting others on their journey of self-discovery, and then to the discovery beyond the self. I love co-exploring the depths of our most guarded secrets, and the heights of our greatest potential. I know that healing the one leads us into an awareness of the other. The only word that I rarely say is the one that I most dearly treasure. It means so many different things to so many different people. But I'll just say it here, and know there are no innate limits to this precious word, only those boundaries that others assign to it for the sake of their own sense of security. Thank you, God, for all aspects of this existence, for this wondrous life, and the love I have known.

Thank you Angela Lauria, so very much for seeing and encouraging me to fully engage in the game of life. To the Morgan James Publishing team: Special thanks to David Hancock, CEO & Founder for believing in me and my message. To my Author Relations Manager, Gayle West, thanks for making the process seamless and easy. Many more thanks to everyone else, but especially Jim Howard, Bethany Marshall, and Nickcole Watkins.

Recommended Books

Train Your Mind Change Your Brain, by Sharon Begley
The Hero's Journey, by Joseph Campbell
The Success Principles, by Jack Canfield
The Emotional Life of Your Brain, by Richard J. Davidson, Ph.D.
Soul Shifts, by Dr. Barbara De Angelis
Breaking the Habit of Being Yourself, by Dr. Joe Dispenza
Men Are from Mars, Women Are from Venus, by Dr. John Gray
The Elegant Universe, by Brian Greene
Buddha's Brain, by Rick Hanson, PhD
The Difference, by Angela E. Lauria
The Art of Living, by Thich Nhat Hanh
Breathe, You Are Alive: Sutra on the Full Awareness of Breathing, by Thich Nhat Hanh
The Heart of the Buddha's Teachings, by Thich Nhat Hanh
You are Here, by Thich Nhat Hanh
Transforming & Healing: Sutra on the Four Establishments of Mindfulness, by Thich Nhat Hanh
Stilling the Mind, by B. Alan Wallace

I am somewhat of a voracious learner and reader, so this is just a drop of the genius of others that I have read. I am so very grateful to all of the authors that contribute to our appreciation and understanding of life.

About the Author

Ron has spent the last fifty years exploring the deepest caves and soaring heights of our personal and spiritual journey. He is intimate with all aspects of the territory. As a guide, he has supported thousands of others on their journey as they've moved through their most difficult challenges and developed their greatest potential.

He was trained by and worked with the best of the best, with early mentors like Joseph Campbell, Buckminster Fuller, and other leaders in the spiritual and personal growth fields.

Rounding out his whole body, mind, and spirit, integrated approach, Ron has earned a Masters in English, a Ph.D. in Transformational Therapy, and a Doctor of Chiropractic degree. Yet Ron feels that his most important credentials have come from the challenges he has overcome on his own journey, and the incredible learning opportunities that life and working with others has offered him.

His service has evolved into working with those committed to their path and the influential leaders who guide them. While there are many who can help you treat the symptoms arising from your challenges, Ron's unique work takes you into and through the deepest source. This empowering approach allows you to make lasting life improvements while transforming those challenges into the greatest opportunities of your life.

If you are looking for the way home, Ron is the transformational guide who can show you the way. Ron lives in Santa Barbara, CA with his lovely wife, Carol.

Thank You

I appreciate you reading this book. I hope it has helped you identify empowering solutions to your challenges while also opening you up to greater possibilities for your life.

FREE VIDEO: To support you on your personal journey, please be my guest for "**A Deeper Look**."

In this complimentary video, we'll explore going within and looking for the deeper source of any challenge. When you're aware of the source, you can start making effective course corrections and stop wasting your time and energy chasing outer symptoms. Go to www.adeeperlookvideo.com

 Morgan James makes all of our titles available
through the Library for All Charity Organization.

www.LibraryForAll.org

Printed in the USA
CPSIA information can be obtained
at www.ICGtesting.com
JSHW082229140824
68134JS00017B/810